Becoming a Woman of Worth

A Biblical Study in Discovering Self Worth

Becky H. Drace

D1379160

Anchor Productions
Jerry Drace Evangelistic Association, Inc.
236 Sanders Bluff Road
Humboldt, TN 38343

ISBN 0-9727404-1-4

Drace, Becky H.
Becoming a Woman of Worth, A Biblical Study in Discovering Self Worth

All Scripture quotations are from the NEW KING JAMES VERSION, THE OPEN BIBLE, 1983,1985, Thomas Nelson Inc. Publishers. All rights reserved. Used by permission.

Cover design by Claire Apple

Dedicated to

Rebecca Lucille Drace

Becoming a Woman of Worth

Table of Contents

Preface

Introduction

WEEK ONE - Transformed 3

    Lesson one - Chosen
    Lesson two - Changed
    Lesson three - Introduction to Fasting
    Lesson four - Called
    Lesson five - Personal Applications - Transformation

WEEK TWO - Commitment 21

    Lesson one - The Woman of Samaria
    Lesson two - The Woman of Samaria, part 2
    Lesson three - Fasting and Prayer - An unbeatable combination
    Lesson four - Observations Regarding Commitment
    Lesson five- Personal Applications - Commitment

WEEK THREE - Wise 41

    Lesson one - Esther
    Lesson two - Esther, part 2
    Lesson three - Praying God's Will
    Lesson four - Observations Regarding Wisdom
    Lesson five - Personal Applications - Wisdom

WEEK FOUR - Submission 57

    Lesson one - Mary Magdalene
    Lesson two - Mary Magdalene, part 2
    Lesson three - A Powerful Prayer Life
    Lesson four - Observations Regarding Submission
    Lesson five - Personal Applications - Submission

WEEK FIVE - Victorious 75

       Lesson one - Hannah
       Lesson two - Hannah, part 2
       Lesson three - A Thankful Heart
       Lesson four - Observations Regarding Victory
       Lesson five - Personal Applications - Victory

WEEK SIX - Devoted 97

       Lesson one - Martha
       Lesson two - Mary
       Lesson three - Sex is Spiritual
       Lesson four - Observations Regarding Devotion
       Lesson five - Personal Applications - Devotion

WEEK SEVEN -Leader 119

       Lesson one - Deborah
       Lesson two - Deborah, part 2
       Lesson three - Living Doubt Free
       Lesson four - Observations Regarding Leadership
       Lesson five - Personal Applications - Leadership

WEEK EIGHT - Consecrated 139

       Lesson one - Dorcas
       Lesson two - Phoebe
       Lesson three - Living the Fast Life
       Lesson four - Observations Regarding Consecration
       Lesson five - Personal Applications - Consecration

Leading a Small Group 155
Teaching Guides..156
Eight Principles on becoming a Woman of Worth..172
Helps for a Powerful Prayer Life...173
Ammunition for the Battle..174
Scripture for Wisdom..175
Scripture for Praise..176
Real questions from Real Women 179

I believe that nothing   happens by accident. When I married Jerry Drace in 1969, I had no idea where life would take us, but I knew God had a plan. His plan for our family was full time evangelism. For several years, I stayed at home with our children, Andrew and Rebecca, and took care of the home and office responsibilities.

After Rebecca entered college, God expanded our ministry. Jerry and I now travel as a team, conducting **HOPE for the HOME** conferences in churches around the world. These conferences address eleven family topics. During these conferences, I lead sessions for women which allows me the opportunity of hearing the stories of women from every avenue of life. I have heard just about everything imaginable and through it all I have learned something. Every woman wants to be valued as a person.

Where do you find personal worth?
How do you build your confidence?
Do you approach life with boldness?
Are you comfortable with who you are?
Are you easily discouraged?
Do you sometimes feel like a failure?

Women of every century have struggled with how to maintain a balanced life and how to be fulfilled as a woman. The women of the Bible are unique and fascinating. Through studying the private lives of the Bible women, I found some to be confident and self assured. The lives of others had been severely bruised by heartache and despair. One was a queen, one a warrior, one demonically possessed and one a hopeless village nobody. All had one thing in common. They had to make a personal decision about God. Every one of the nine women of this study discovered that contentment, confidence and completion comes as an overflow of the blessing of knowing God personally. Discovering His Will and following Him is the foundation to discovering personal worth.

My prayer for you is that through **<u>Becoming a Woman of Worth</u>** you will learn that God wants you to be part of His Kingdom Plan. I pray that you will submit to the authority of God, and will allow Him to develop your talents and abilities. As you trust Him, you will become more confident and capable. As the challenges of life arise, you will be able to walk through each one, assured of victory. When you discover how valuable you are to God, you have found the simple answer to one of life's most complex issues.

God can take an ordinary woman, just like you to accomplish an extraordinary task. If you are willing, He will fill your life with His love and power. What He asks is that you daily search His Word. As you uncover the treasures that He has recorded in the Bible, you will find the sweet peace of His presence continually assures you that you are indeed a...........

Woman of Worth

Knowing that you are a **Woman of Worth** is a legacy that can influence your children, grandchildren and generations beyond...........

God bless you as you begin your spiritual adventure which I pray will revolutionize your concept of who you are in Christ.

Becky H. Drace

INTRODUCTION

In 1981, while in South Korea, I met a woman who introduced me to a spiritual discipline that I knew very little about. She fasted regularly and shared with me how it brought her into a closer communion with God. Since I knew so little about fasting, after I returned home, I began to dig into the scripture to learn everything I could about the subject. I found that it was practiced throughout the Old Testament and that Jesus taught about fasting. I began to fast periodically, then two years ago, in 2000, I began to fast weekly.

I have found fasting to add a dimension to my Christian walk that I never thought possible. Fasting makes me focus completely on my relationship with God. I have found that I am more aware of the Holy Spirit's presence and it enhances my praise and worship with Christ. I seem to have a greater sensitivity to how God is working in the lives of people around me.

As I was writing this study, I felt that fasting should be studied and combined with prayer. The fast will be the day of your choice but is written in the material to be from after the evening meal on day # 2 until the evening meal on day # 3. This places the day of fasting in the middle of the study week. During the days of fast you will study:

I. The Purpose and Practice of Fasting
    A. Develop an intimacy with God
    B. Change personal focus
    C. Increase your daily awareness of God
II. Praying God's Will
    A. God's Specific Will
        1. Salvation for everyone
        2. A thankful heart
        3. Pure in sexual attitudes
    B. God's Directive Will
        1. Obedience to His Word
        2. Faith to trust His direction

III. Hindrances to a Powerful Prayer Life
    A. Selfish motives
    B. Sinful behavior
    C. Doubt
IV. Living the Fast Life
    A. The connection with prayer
    B. The connection with the Word
    C. The leadership of the Holy Spirit

Fasting will be a new experience for many of you. It can become a time of inspiration and renewal. It will add spice to your spiritual experience. Fasting focuses on disciplining your body both physically and spiritually.

Each week you will study a different aspect of becoming a **Woman of Worth.** Included is a biblical principle and memory verse to support the study and daily homework to encourage you to think about what you believe.

<u>Becoming a Woman of Worth</u>

    1. Transformed
    2. Committed
    3. Wise
    4. Submissive
    5. Victorious
    6. Devoted
    7. Leader
    8. Consecrated

The Holy Spirit will teach you the treasures of God.

There is power in the Word and when prayer and fasting are combined with the Word, you can expect to reach a new level of intimacy with Christ.

Becoming
a
Woman of Worth

WEEK # 1

TRANSFORMED

BECOMING A WOMAN OF WORTH

TRANSFORMED

Week # 1- Lesson #1

MEMORY VERSE

Romans 12:2

"and do not be conformed to this world, but be transformed by the renewing of your mind, that you may prove what is that good and acceptable and perfect will of God."

Principle: Transformation is a process!

This week you will look at what it means to be **chosen** by God, **changed** by His Son, Jesus Christ and **called** for His purpose. You will study the basics of fasting and then take a spiritual evaluation.

Read: II Thessalonians 2:13-14

To be **chosen** means that God wanted you to be part of His family before you were ever born. He wanted you to receive the gift of salvation offered by His son, Jesus Christ. Now He wants you to grow and to become influential in helping others to know Him as you do.

To be sanctified according to the **Great Encyclopedic Dictionary** means to be set apart for holy purposes. In other words it means to be **changed.** Being set apart is a state of growing and changing.

Every individual both male and female has been **called** to be part of the expansion of the Kingdom of God by being a living and verbal witness.

Psalm 139: 13-16 "For You have formed my inward parts. You have covered me in my mother's womb. I will praise You for I am fearfully and wonderfully made. Marvelous are Your works, and that my soul knows very well. My frame was not hidden from You when I was made in secret, and skillfully wrought in the lowest parts of the earth. Your eyes saw my substance, being yet unformed. In your book they all were written. The days fashioned for me, when as yet there were none of them."

3

CHOSEN

The young woman was dark and beautiful. She looked confident and successful. She was dressed in the latest style and exuded an air of assurance. She said, "I'm such a loser! I can't do anything right. Why doesn't God care about me? I don't think He is listening."

What comment do you have regarding this woman's self esteem? What would you tell her about being **chosen?** _____

Ephesians 1:4 "..... He chose us in Him before the foundation of the world, that we should be holy and without blame before Him in love."

What you believe about yourself says more about your spiritual condition than you can imagine. Actually it will reveal what you truly believe about God, Jesus and the Holy Spirit. No one likes to look into the inner being. It is revealing, convicting and challenging. Sometimes it is painful. To become a **Woman of Worth** it is necessary.

As you examine your life alongside what God says in His Word, then you must decide whether you will act on His Word. As you trust His Word and obediently surrender to His authority, you will begin to experience the results of a life full of confidence. The more confident you become in your relationship with Christ, the more you will grow into a self assured **Woman of Worth**.

Read **Psalm 139:13-16.** Write your thoughts.

vs. 13 - _____

vs. 14 - _____

vs. 15 - _____

vs. 16 - _____

4

Many women cannot see themselves as **chosen** because of their past. Be assured that everyone has a past! Your past is one reason you are the way you are. Your past influences the way you react and respond in particular ways and perceive things in a certain manner. Family experiences, birth order, dating habits, marriage relationships, etc. all combine to form us into who we are.

Some women have lost their sense of worth because of present situations. Their dignity may have been damaged by their lifestyle. They may feel guilty because of mistakes. Feelings of guilt can become a breeding ground for discouragement and depression.

There is one area, however, that must be placed in a higher position than all of your past or your present. That is how you perceive yourself in light of who Jesus is. He loves you. More than any love you have ever experienced. Think of the greatest love you could ever know and then place above that the love of Christ. Only the love of Jesus can give you personal worth!

As you claim God's Word and pray to become a **Woman of Worth,** you will begin to see the value of your life. You will notice changes in your attitude toward yourself and others.

Making scripture personal helps you to know God intimately.

Read **John 3:16.** Write and personalize this verse._____

_____

Read **John 10:10.** What would be your interpretation of this verse? _____

_____

As you close Lesson #1, write a prayer of praise and thanksgiving to God for choosing you.

_____

_____

_____

CHANGED

The first step in becoming a **Woman of Worth** is to know that you are chosen. The second step is growing and changing. This is the phase of greatest neglect. It takes discipline to grow. Sometimes it is painful to change. It may mean making difficult choices regarding habits, attitudes, behavior and friends.

II Corinthians 5:17

"Therefore, if anyone is in Christ, he is a new creation; old things have passed away; behold all things have become new."

Read: **II Corinthians 5:17.**

The concept is metamorphosis: " **to change**".

Metamorphosis is defined as "Complete transformation of character, purpose, circumstances, etc." Meta means "change". Morph means "having the form of" and osis means the "process". So to be a new creature in Christ is to take on His form, to be changed into His image and continue in this process for life.

Do you know that you cannot change yourself? Only Christ can change you!

Phil 1:6 "being confident of this very thing, that He who has begun a good work in you will complete it until the day of Jesus Christ."

Evaluate your attitudes and habits. Are you consistent in your relationship with Jesus? Do you have a daily time of study and prayer? What are your priorities? Do you have friends that encourage your spiritual growth?

List areas where you feel change is needed in your life?_____

_____

_____

Are you willing to allow Christ to bring a change into your life?_____

Do you see yourself as a temple in which Christ dwells?

> **I Corinthians 6:19**
>
> "Do you not know that your body is the temple of the Holy Spirit who is in you, whom you have from God, and you are not your own?"

Think of the beautiful places of worship in the world. How are they furnished? What makes a house of worship special?

_____

_____

For **change** to take place, you must strengthen every area of your life. Your heart, mind, soul and body need to be seen as a residence of God. You must come under the authority and control of the Holy Spirit.

Change comes with a price. The price is time. Time to study must be given each day. It has to be a priority. Seek verses that help you in the areas of your weakness. Read these verses daily so they will take root in your life and then daily allow them to grow in your heart. Your mind will begin to perceive life from the viewpoint of God as you daily receive instruction from His Word. Select a passage for memory that you can quote when you feel weak or need reassurance.

Samples of scripture for memory:
> **I Corinthians 6:19-20**
> **II Corinthians 5:17**
> **Mark 12: 30-31**
> **Romans 12:1-2**

Write your selected verse on an index card. Keep it as a reminder of the presence of God. Write these selected verses and add a personal comment.

_____

_____

Remember: **Inconsistent Christian growth becomes a breeding ground for doubt and sin.**

Developing a strong prayer life is another essential in the metamorphosis of your heart and soul. Jesus' prayer life serves as an example of how to develop a powerful and active prayer life.

Study the prayer life of Jesus

Luke 5: 16 "So He Himself often withdrew into the wilderness and prayed."	**Luke 6:12** - For guidance in making decisions. **John 11:41-42** - Resurrection of Lazarus **Luke 9:28-29** - At the transfiguration **Luke 10: 1-24** - During evangelization and salvation **Luke 22:39-40** - For strength during temptation **John 17** - The model prayer **Matthew 26:26-27** - Before meals **Luke 23:34** - On the cross **Matthew 14:19; Mark 6:41; Luke 9:16 John 6:11** - Before miracles

John 11:1-2 "It came to pass, as He was praying in a certain place, when He ceased, that one of His disciples said to Him, "Lord, teach us to pray, as John also taught his disciples. Then He said to them, "WHEN YOU PRAY..."

A certain place - Prayer must be specific
A certain time - Prayer must be a priority
Consistency - Prayer must be a regular part of life

Jesus' prayer life was comfortable. He talked with His father. He communed. Commune is defined as *"to converse or confer intimately"*. Your goal in prayer is to grow an intimate relationship with God through Jesus. Become comfortable talking and listening in your prayer time.

To close Lesson # 2 spend time in prayer. Write your thoughts.

_____

_____

Fast from the evening meal today until the evening meal tomorrow. Tomorrow you will begin to study fasting.

FASTING

The day of fast is scheduled to be from after the evening meal on Tuesday until the evening meal on Wednesday. However, you may wish to select another day for fasting. If you have health concerns, check with your physician for advice in developing this discipline. Begin a journal to record your thoughts.

Along with studying the Bible and developing a prayer life, another

> **Matthew 6:16** "WHEN you fast, do not be like the hypocrites, with a sad countenance, for they disfigure their faces that they may appear to men to be fasting. Assuredly, I say to you, they have their reward. BUT you, when you fast, anoint your head and wash your face, so that you do not appear to men to be fasting, but to your Father who is in the secret place and your Father who sees in secret will reward you openly."

discipline is fasting. Fasting was considered part of the regular rituals of the religious community of Jesus day. However, fasting is taught throughout the Bible as a most significant part of the Christian walk.

Consider this: We spend more on food, eat more food, discard more food, and weigh more because of our eating habits than most every country and people on earth. Did you know that in the city of San Francisco, California, there are enough restaurants to seat every resident at the same time?

I Corinthians 9:27 "I discipline my body and bring it unto subjection lest, when I have preached to others, I myself should become a negative witness."

Write your thoughts on this verse._____

_____

As you begin your fast, pray that your day will be focused on feeding your spirit instead of your body. You will find an amazing change taking place. In place of physical food, give your spirit a boost. When you feel hungry, read your memory verse and then pray and ask the Lord to feed you from His Word.

Have you previously experienced fasting? _____

Have you known of individuals who have fasted as a part of their spiritual discipline?

_____

_____

Seldom do we "make" our bodies do as we choose for spiritual reasons. Fasting offers you that challenge.

Reasons to develop the spiritual discipline of fasting:

1. It is practiced throughout the Bible.
2. Jesus spoke about fasting on several occasions.
3. Fasting will help you focus centrally on spiritual matters.
4. Fasting takes the focus off physical food and places it on spiritual food.
5. Fasting can help you be more sensitive to global hunger.

During these days of fasting, you will study how to have a more powerful prayer life. You will examine reasons why your prayer time may be lacking in power and discover how to strengthen your daily walk.

When you join in a prayer union with others to pray for something specific, you have entertwined to create a force that is more powerful than dynamite. Prayer can weaken the power of Satan. Prayer can shake the foundation of hell. Prayer can result in the salvation of the lost. Prayer can break the bondage of sin. When believers have united in prayer, history has been changed and armies have been defeated.

You can not contain the power of a praying Christian.

Select a prayer partner who will join you in fasting and prayer during this eight week study. Write a prayer of encouragement in your journal.

Read **Matthew 18:20.** Write your thoughts. _____

_____

Read the examples of fasting on page 9. End your day in prayer.

As you study these verses, make notes on your thoughts.

Occasions for fasting:
    I Samuel 1:7_____
    I Samuel 7:5-6_____
    I Samuel 31:11-13_____
    II Samuel 12:16_____
    Nehemiah 1:4_____
    Esther 4:16_____
    Daniel 6:18-20_____
    Acts 13:3_____

Accompaniments for fasting:
    Nehemiah 9:1-2 _____
    Joel 2:12 _____
    Luke 2: 37 _____

Safeguards for fasting:
    Psalm 35:13_____
    Psalm 69:10_____
    Isaiah 58:1-14_____
    Zechariah 7:5-7_____
    Matthew 6:16-18 _____

Results of fasting:
    Judges 20:26-28_____
    Matthew 4:1-11_____

Examples of fasting:
Exodus 34:27-28_____	Judges 20:26_____
I Kings 19:2,8 _____	II Samuel 12:16_____
Nehemiah 1:4_____	Jonah 3:5-6_____
Daniel 9:3_____	Daniel 6:9,18_____
Matthew 4:1,2_____	Luke 2:36,37_____
Acts 13:2_____	Mark 2:18_____
II Corinthians 11:27_____	II Corinthians 6:4,5_____

Record your thoughts on fasting._____

_____

_____

As you feed your spirit, you will become more sensitive.

While you are fasting, ask for God's awareness regarding those around you. Pray for your family. Are each of your family members saved and living for Christ? How can you pray for each of your family members? Write your prayer plans in your journal.

Pray for your friends. What is their spiritual status? Are you involved in friendships which may tempt you to compromise your faith? How can you be a witness to your friends?

> **Philippians 4:6**
>
> "Be anxious for nothing, but in everything by prayer and supplication, with thanksgiving, let your requests be made known unto God."

Do you know your neighbors and your co-workers? Has someone taken you into their confidence? How can you encourage them? How will you pray for those in need?

Ask that God make you sensitive to those around you as you develop this aspect of your spiritual disciplines.

(A detailed study of fasting will be included in the weeks to come).

To close this lesson on fasting, write your thoughts and some of your prayer requests. _____

_____

_____

_____

_____

CALLED

The third step in becoming a **Woman of Worth** is to realize that you are **called.** Being called means realizing that you have purpose.

Do you know that you have a purpose in life besides being a woman, student, wife, mother, friend and having a career? Many women find their worth in one or more of these areas? You have been called to a higher purpose which should be reflective in every area of womanhood.

You are special!

You are chosen!

You are changed!

You are called!

"I feel more important at work than at home. At work I am in charge. I am a Vice President and make important decisions every day. People ask my opinion. I am a professional business woman. I think my purpose is to be as good as I can at my job. Besides, at work I can forget everything for a while and concentrate on being successful."

What is the problem with this definition of "purpose"?_____

What is your purpose?_____

Where do you find affirmation? _____

In what activity do you spend the majority of your time?_____

You will find time for what you consider most important!

Your first calling is to have fellowship with God through His son, Jesus.

How do you plan to grow in fellowship with Jesus?_____

_____

I Corinthians 1:9

"God is faithful by whom you were called into the fellowship of His Son, Jesus Christ our Lord."

Will you make a commitment to daily growth? _____
Have a friend sign and date your commitment.

Sign _____ Date _____

1. God will reveal Himself to you through His Word.
2. When you study the life of Jesus, you learn more about God.
3. God will speak to you through your prayer time.
4. The Holy Spirit will become a strong presence as you seek to know more about Him and His work in your life.

The more determined you are in developing your relationship with the Lord, the more your life will take on the image of Christ and the more you will hunger after the things of God.

Your second calling is to live a life that is different from the norm.

I John 1: 3

"that which we have seen and heard we declare to you, that you also may have fellowship with us and truly our fellowship is with the Father and with His Son, Jesus Christ."

Your goal should be to become an example that will lead other people to have a desire to know God as you do and to have a relationship with Him as you have.

What would be a normal reaction to stress, difficulty, sin, death, financial loss, marital strife, rebellious children, relationship problems, or job challenges?

Often there is no difference between the way an unbeliever reacts to lifes' challenges and the way a Christian reacts to lifes' challenges. When you grasp the concept of "a higher calling", then you will **want** to react in a Christ like manner.

Ephesians 1: 17

"that the God of our Lord Jesus Christ, the Father of glory, may give to you the spirit of wisdom and revelation in the knowledge of Him. The eyes of your understanding being enlightened that you may know what is the hope of His calling, what are the riches of the glory of His inheritance in the saints and what is the exceeding greatness of His power toward us who believe according to the working of His mighty power."

What do you think this verse is saying to you?_____

_____

The call on the life of a Christian is to holy living.
The call on the life of a Christian is to make wise decisions.
The call on the life of a Christian is to be thankful.
The call on the life of a Christian is to be content.
The call on the life of a Christian is to be like Christ.
The call on the life of a Christian is to be an example in the faith.
The call on the life of a Christian is to bring honor to God.
The call on the life of a Christian is to remain faithful.
The call on the life of a Christian is to be consistent.

Can you think of other aspects of being called to the inheritance of Christ?

Read **Ephesians 1:18**.
Write your thoughts. To what does this inheritance refer?

_____

_____

_____

Your inheritance is the riches of glory and the abundance of daily living!

15

Personal Applications - Transformed

This week you have studied the basic principles and concepts of being transformed into a **Woman of Worth.**

Many women do not live their lives with an active faith. In order to live as Paul says "in Christ" you must discipline your life and become consistent in your fellowship with Him.

Ephesians 2:10
"For we are His workmanship, created in Christ Jesus for good works, which God prepared beforehand that we should walk in them."

---

1. To become a **Woman of Worth** you must believe that you are **special**!

2. To become a **Woman of Worth** will be a life long process of transformation. Transformation comes from daily pursuing a personal relationship with Jesus Christ.

2. To become a **Woman of Worth** you must believe that you were **chosen** before the world was formed. God knows your name and He has a special plan for your life.

3. To become a **Woman of Worth** you must believe that you are in the process of being **changed** into the image of Jesus Christ. As your relationship with Him grows, you will begin to have changed attitudes. You will be able to pinpoint areas where you need to grow.

4. To become a **Woman of Worth** you must believe that you are **called** to a higher purpose than ordinary existence. Your purpose is to have fellowship with God through His son, Jesus Christ, and to lead other people in your sphere of influence to know that they, too, have a purpose in life.

Take a moment to evaluate how you feel about your self worth. Write down your feelings. Be specific._____

Take the personal spiritual survey on page 15.

Over 200 years ago, John Wesley used these questions as a devotional guide for the members of his class. Make notes of the ones which are areas of weakness in your life.

1. Am I consciously or unconsciously creating the impression that I am a better person than I really am? In other words, am I a hypocrite?

2. Am I honest in all my acts and words, or do I exaggerate?

3. Do I confidentially pass on what was told me in confidence? Can I be trusted?

4. Am I a slave to dress, friends, work or habit?

5. Am I self-conscious, self-pitying or self-justifying?

6. Did the Bible live in me today?

7. Do I give the Bible time to speak to me everyday?

8. Am I enjoying prayer?

9. When did I last speak to someone else of my faith?

10. Do I pray about the money I spend?

11. Do I get to bed on time and get up on time?

12. Do I disobey God in anything?

13. Do I insist on doing something about which my conscience is uneasy?

14. Am I defeated in any part of my life?

15. Am I jealous, impure, irritable, touchy, or distrustful?

16. How do I spend my spare time?

17. Am I proud?

18. Do I thank God I am not as others (as the Pharisee who despised the publican)?

19. Is there anyone I fear or dislike, or criticize, or resent? If so, what am I doing about it?

20. Is Christ real to me?

To become a **Woman of Worth** you must trust, obey, and make a commitment to be consistent in your daily walk-of-faith. God has a plan for your life, but it is up to you to follow His plan. You will choose to follow Him or not.

You must trust that God's Word is true and that He has your best interests before Him at all times.
You must be willing to obey His word.
You must be willing to make personal life changing commitments.

Many women never meet their potential in Christ because of their refusal to view life from God's perspective. Dwelling on the past keeps you from being able to move forward in God's grace, mercy and goodness.

Read **Exodus 14:12**. Write your thoughts. _____

_____

In the book of Exodus, we read where the children of Israel decided they had rather live as slaves in Egypt rather than let God lead them to the promised land. They had developed a taste for rich food, ungodly living and unrighteousness. They were comfortable living and worshipping as pagans.

Some women have adopted this same mind set. They have become comfortable with their present lifestyles. They had rather live an **ordinary** life than accept the challenge of allowing God to change their lives for eternity and reveal to them an **extraordinary** way to live.

God wants your life to be filled with all the treasures of His kingdom. He will show Himself to you as you seek to know Him.

A prayer to end your week: Lord, thank You for Your goodness. Thank You for Your great love. Please let me, (your name here), sense Your presence today. Reveal to me Your greatness and allow me to know that I am special to You. Please open Your Word to me so that I may experience a change in my attitude today. Please place someone across my path today who needs a special touch from You.

In the name of Your Son, I pray.

Becoming
a
Woman of Worth

WEEK # 2

COMMITTED

BECOMING A WOMAN OF WORTH

COMMITTED

MEMORY VERSE

John 4: 14

"Whoever drinks of the water that I shall give him will never thirst. But the water that I shall give him will become in him a fountain of water springing up into ever lasting life."

Principle: Commitment begins with faith!

The woman of Samaria is a perfect example of what it means to be **chosen, changed** and **called** for His purpose. As you study her encounter with Jesus, place yourself in the picture.

Read: **John 4:4-39**

John 4:4 - "He needed to go through Samaria"

What does it mean that Jesus **needed** to go through Samaria?_____

_____

The land of Samaria was the shortest route from Jerusalem to Galilee, but the Jews would not go through their land. The Samaritan people were outcasts. The rivalry between the Jews and Samaritans extended back to the days of the patriarchs. It was a long running problem. The Samaritans were non-existent as far as the Jews were concerned. Furthermore, men would not normally become engaged in conversation with a strange woman, especially a Samaritan woman.

Jesus readily began a conversation with the woman.

Did Jesus just by chance end up at the well at noon? Jesus always has a purpose in everything and every encounter. The woman was hoping to get her bucket filled and then quietly slip back into her life of emptiness.

Why had the woman chosen this time of day to go to the well of Sychar?

It was the hottest part of the day. Normally the women of the village would come in the cool of the morning or the cool of the late afternoon for water. They would probably have come in a group as friends, visiting along the way, catching up on family and work and the latest news from town. Why would this woman choose to come during the heat of the noonday sun, alone?

From what was she hiding? Who or what was she avoiding?

Mark 1:35
"Now in the morning having risen a long while before daylight, He went out and departed to a solitary place and there He prayed."

Have you ever wanted to be all alone? Some times solitude is good. When you withdraw in order to renew your fellowship with God, it is good.

Read **Mark 1:35; Luke 9:18**. Write your comment.

_____

_____

_____

This woman was avoiding contact with the other women of the village. Perhaps she was afraid of their comments and looks of disdain. Maybe she was ashamed of her life. Perhaps she was discouraged or even depressed. She had a bad reputation with the other villagers. She was perhaps hiding from the looks of accusation and a feeling of guilt because of her past. She probably had lost faith in believing that any good thing would come her way. She must have believed that her life was worthless and that her destiny was to be no more than a simple village nobody. She knew she was an outcast and her possibilities were grim.

> **Everyone has a past. Your past is part of the reason you are the way you are. Your value system, outlook on life and family history are all important pieces of the picture of your life. However, your past is only part of who you are!**

Your past can become a great asset to becoming what God wants you to be. Your weaknesses can become strengths. Your past hurts and sadnesses can be used of God in the most amazing ways.

> **I Thessalonians 5:16-18**
>
> "Rejoice always, pray without ceasing, in everything give thanks; for this is the will of God in Christ Jesus for you."

Take time to thank God for your past! Many women cannot move forward in Christ because of their past mistakes. Give your past to Jesus right now!

John 4:6 - "Jesus, therefore being wearied from His journey, sat by the well."

Did you ever think of Jesus being tired? Jesus was all human and all divine. He experienced everything just like you. Exhaustion was part of His day, too. How do you react when you are tired? Even though Jesus was physically weary, He made time for others. He knew the woman would be at the well. He knew she would be bitter, sad, searching, empty and in desperate need of being filled.

She came with an empty bucket to draw water from a running well. She also came with an empty life needing to be filled with eternal living water.

Jesus **"sat"**. Jesus is never in a hurry when you are in need. He will always be available to sit with you and meet you right where you are. He met the woman where she was hurting.

Jesus came to her personally and privately!

Why did Jesus send his disciples off to town for food?_____

The thirst of the body can always be quenched by a cool drink of water. Nothing quenches like water. Yet, only living water can quench the thirst of a hurting spirit. Jesus took the opportunity at hand to present to this woman a way to have a new life.

He knew that her heart was filled with pain and despair. He knew that she was consumed with misery and her guilt had her spiraling out of control.

John 4:7 "Give me a drink"

John 4:8 "How is it that you, a Jew, ask for a drink from me, a Samaritan woman?"

Jesus didn't have a dipper or a bucket. Was the main reason for this question His thirst or her need?

_____

John 4:8 "How is it that you, a Jew, ask for a drink from me, a Samaritan woman?" Besides you don't even have a dipper and the well is deep!"

How does her response reveal how she felt about who she was?

_____

John 4:10 "If you only knew.... you would ask and He would give you living water."

The first comment from Jesus addresses her reasoning.

Her reasoning said, "I am a woman, He is a man. I am a Samaritan. He is a Jew. I have a dipper, and yet He is offering me water." She reasoned that she could get a satisfying drink from the well of her forefathers at any time.

John 4:13 "Whoever drinks of this water will thirst again, but whoever drinks of the water that I shall give, will never thirst again and it will become a fountain of water springing up into everlasting life."

24

Jesus opens up to her an eternal idea. It is possible to have water that satisfies for eternity. Is it possible for her, a Samaritan woman to be **chosen** to drink this "living water" and then to be a fountain of water for others?

John 4:15 "Sir, give me this water, that I may not thirst, nor come here to draw."

What do you think the woman is thinking?_____

_____

The second comment from Jesus addresses her relationships.

John 4:16 "Go, call your husband, and come here."

Read **John 4:16-18.** How did Jesus handle her past and present?

Did he condemn her? _____

What did the woman think about Jesus ability to know her life?_____

_____

In addressing her relationships, Jesus opens up to the woman the possibility of **change.** Her past and present circumstances were acknowledged by Jesus to reveal to her His power and authority to know her as a person all the way into the personal parts of her daily life. How could He know these things?_____

_____

Did the woman make any excuses or try to explain her relationships? _____

_____

Why did she respond so openly to Jesus?_____

The third comment from Jesus addresses religion.

John 4:19-24 Read these verses and write your thoughts.

_____

_____

_____

_____

     John 4:23-24 "the hour is coming, and now is, when the true worshipers will worship the Father in spirit and truth: for the Father is seeking such to worship Him. God is Spirit, and those who worship Him must worship in spirit and truth."

     In addressing her concepts of religion, Jesus revealed the true meaning of worship. He reveals to her that He is the Messiah. He reveals to her His power and authority. He uses her reasoning, relationships, and religious ideas to reach into her life to show her how she could change for eternity. All of a sudden, her life has meaning and purpose. She has realized that she is indeed, **chosen.**

     Read **John 4:26** Write what these verses say about the woman's reaction to her encounter with Jesus. How did she come to this decision? _____

_____

_____

_____

> **John 4: 23b** "...for the Father is seeking such to worship Him."

The woman of Samaria went to the well not only physically thirsty but spiritually starving for a drink of eternal water. Being desperate and with no hope, filled with unanswered questions, she received answers that satisfied her spiritual starvation. She went back into town with a new life and with an eternal assurance that her encounter with the Messiah, Jesus Christ, had given her "living water". Do you think she took a drink of the water from the well?

Read **John 4: 39** How do you know that a "fountain of living water" was overflowing from the woman?_____

_____

As you close your study today, think of your life and the lives of those around you.

Pray for a sensitive heart for God. Ask for a new sense of God's presence in your life.

As you begin your fast today, write your prayer concerns._____

_____

_____

_____

_____

_____

A prayer for you: Oh Lord, I worship You as God in control of everything. You are the revealer of past, present and future. Thank You for Your Son, Jesus, our Messiah. Thank You for Your Spirit and for Your truth. Please reveal to me Your truth so that my life may bring honor to You.

27

FASTING AND PRAYER - An unbeatable combination

As you develop the discipline of fasting you will become more aware of your relationship with God through Jesus Christ. The presence of the Holy Spirit will become more apparent to you as you move through your daily activities.

Last week we studied the basic information regarding fasting throughout the Bible. These passages revealed, by the example of others, the importance of fasting and the results from fasting. We also began a prayer and fast journal to record thoughts and experiences. This week we will examine the purpose and practice of fasting.

> **Romans 15:4** "For whatever things were written before were written for our learning, that we through the patience and comfort of the Scriptures might have hope."

1. Fast to develop an intimacy with God.

Many people believe "in" God but are not intimate "with" God. The difference can be explained by comparing looking at a painting of a beautiful landscape versus walking in the place of the painting and experiencing all the sights, smells, wonders, and beauty in the painting.

Developing an intimate relationship with God should be the goal of every believer. However, before you can be intimate with God you must have a relationship with His son, Jesus.

Read **John 1:1-14** and write your thoughts on these verses.

_____

_____

_____

_____

Where were you when you became aware of your need to know Jesus as Savior and Lord? How did you respond to this need?_____

_____

What changes have occurred in your life since you became a believer in Jesus Christ? How is your life different today than it was yesterday, last week or last year?_____

_____

What benefits have you experienced because of your relationship with Christ?

_____

_____

_____

Do you agree that as a Christian, your goal should be to become consistent in your growth in Christ. What steps do you take to insure a growing relationship with God?

_____

STEPS TO SALVATION

Know that you have a need to know God
Know that Jesus is God's only son and your Savior
Acknowledge that you are unacceptable to God because of sin
Be willing to release your sin to Jesus
Believe in your heart that Jesus died for you and lives again
Confess with your life that He is Lord
Commit your life daily to Christ

Pray a prayer of rejoicing for your salvation.

2. Fast to change your personal focus.

Most of our focus is on physical needs. Food, appearance, fashion and personal desires are such an overwhelming part of our culture that it has become a priority in our personal habits. When you spend time in fasting it places the emphasis on what you need spiritually rather than what you desire physically.

Take time to evaluate your priorities.

1. How important is physical appearance to you?
2. How much time do you spend preparing to "be presentable"?
3. How much of your time is spent on physical needs?
4. How important is food to your day?
5. What consumes most of your thoughts each day?

As you fast, you are disciplining your body to submit to a period of time spent concentrating on the development of your spiritual life.

Replace the physical yearning for food with food from God's word.
When you feel hungry spend time reading and memorizing a verse.
Listen to praise music as much as possible during the day.
Make a list of your prayer concerns then pray for one specifically.
Write three reasons you feel blessed today.
Record your experiences during the day.

Wonderful benefits come from a regular discipline of fasting. You will come to know God in a fresh way. You will have a greater sense of His presence during the hours of your fast. You will also find that combining fasting and prayer with your daily study will bring a new clarity to scripture and a greater awareness of the presence of the Holy Spirit as your teacher.

Just as the life of the woman of Samaria was changed because of her personal encounter with Jesus, so your life will change as you pursue a deeper relationship with Jesus.

3. Fast to increase your awareness of God on a daily basis.

Most of the day is spent doing routine things. How aware of the presence of God are you during your daily activities? _____

As you concentrate on your relationship with God, you will find that you are more aware of your dependence on Him. Your interactions with other people, your reaction to daily frustrations, your appreciation for the blessings of life, will all be affected by your deepening awareness of His presence in your life.

Do you know that there is no place you can go to escape the presence of God? How will you depend on God to meet your needs today? _____

Take a moment to enjoy nature. Just rest for a moment in the awesome beauty of God's creation. He made the world for you to enjoy and eyes for you to see and behold the wonders of His creation. He made you with ears to hear music. Have you thought of the intricate details in the world that God has designed?

Listen to hear something that reminds you of God's gift of sound.

Look for something special today that reminds you of God's goodness.

Which color has stood out to you today?

Find and write one verse as a reminder of God's mercy.

The combination of fasting and prayer will become a regular part of your week. You will look forward to the time spent concentrating on your relationship with God and feeding your spirit with food from the heart of God.

End this day by reading and meditating on **Psalm 104** and write your comments.

_____

_____

_____

Observations Regarding Commitment

The woman of Samaria reveals a woman who was willing to make a **commitment**. Her main problem was not her reasoning, relationships nor religion, it was her lack of being able to make a commitment.

In our society it is easy to get out of commitments. We begin a new class, but fail to finish it. We get married, then decide it was a wrong decision. We make a new friend, but do not nurture the friendship. We attend church when we feel like it, but do not get involved.

Why do you feel that commitments are often hard to keep?_____

_____

Where would you be today if Jesus had decided that the price to be paid was to great for Him and He decided not to follow through with His commitment to you?_____

Romans 5:8 "God demonstrated His love for you in that while you were still a sinner, Christ died for you."

An indecisive person is often insecure in who they are and what their purpose is in life. Often they will cover up these emotions by trying to appear self assured and in control. The Samaritan woman is an example of lack of commitment. She was afraid, confused, misdirected, and non committed. Her remarks indicate she wanted to appear confident and self assured.

Read **John 4:11-12; 19-20**

Do you cover up personal fears and insecurities? If so what emotions do you use to appear confident and self assured?_____

_____

Maintaining your commitment will take time, energy, and involvement.

> **Hebrews 12:2** "... looking unto Jesus, the author and the finisher of our faith, who for the joy that was set before Him endured the cross, despising the shame, and has sat down at the right hand of the throne of God. Consider Him who endured such hostility from sinners against Himself, lest you become weary and discouraged in your souls."

The woman's previous commitments were shallow based on her misunderstanding of her reasoning, her religious practices and her past relationships.

Four thoughts on the Woman of Samaria's inability to commit.

1. She reasoned that her heritage would give her purpose in life.

2. The problems in her personal relationships caused guilt and out of the guilt arose a feeling of lack of self worth resulting in her avoidance of others.

3. Her religious practices became an excuse for not living righteously.

4. Her cultural bigotry was a barrier to her finding purpose.

How the woman came to believe she was **special.**

1. She asked the right questions.
2. She realized her need.
3. She exercised her faith.
4. She trusted in the words of Jesus.
5. She opened her life to the transforming power of Jesus Christ.
6. She was willing to become "living water" in the lives of others.
7. She was bold in relating her experience with Jesus.

> **John 4: 39** "And many of the Samaritans of that city believed in Him because of the word of the woman who testified. 'He told me all that I ever did'."

The woman of Samaria shows the transformation of a woman who felt she was worth nothing into a woman of commitment and purpose.

Review the Samaritan woman's experience with Jesus.

Your thoughts are very important. How you observe Jesus' interaction and involvement is key to how you perceive your own experience with Jesus. Use this page to write your thoughts on the transition of her life once she encountered Jesus.

John 4:1-39 _____

_____

_____

_____

_____

_____

_____

As you close this day, begin with a time of renewal and recommitment of your personal relationship with Jesus. Pray for your personal requests.

Write and date your prayer. _____

_____

_____

Personal Applications - Commitment

Today will be a day of personal introspection and application of the experience of the Woman of Samaria. Before you can become a **Woman of Worth** you must be willing to make a permanent **commitment** to your spiritual growth. Just as we need the proper stimulation to grow physically, we need stimulation to grow spiritually.

In order for "living water" to continue to flow as a fountain from your life, you must draw from the deep well of the presence of God, from the wisdom of His Word, and be involved in the fellowship of believers through a local bible teaching church. As you grow, you will learn more about the Holy Spirit, who He is and what He does for you. As you are willing to commit more areas of your life to Him, you will become "living water" flowing into the lives of others.

What would keep a fountain from being able to flow?_____

_____

_____

    1. Debris can keep water from flowing. Is there debris in your life?

    What are your daily priorities? Are there activities in your life which are taking too much of your time? _____

    Evaluate the activity of your last three days and record your time line by the hour. (You may need to use additional paper for this time evaluation.)

_____

_____

    How can you make better use of your time? Do you have a systematic regular study and prayer time?

2. Rocks in the stream can hamper the flow of water.

Sometimes the rocks in the stream are tiny, but even the tiniest of rocks, when stacked on top of each other can dam up the flow of water. At other times the rocks are boulders which seem immovable and inhibit the flow of water.

Do you have rocks in the stream of your life that keep you from being able to experience the power of the Lord? Is there something that you have kept hidden that needs to be exposed so that the "living water" can flow freely as a fountain? Are there pebbles in your life which have now become a stack of stones that hinder the flow? Are there boulders which have become a stronghold and have ensnared your emotions? Are you fearful, anxious, or preoccupied with insignificant thoughts? Are you blaming your past and allowing the boulder of past experiences to keep you from having a deep relationship with the Lord?

Write any thoughts that have come to your mind. _____

_____

_____

_____

_____

3. Mud and silt often become so thick that the water flow is cloudy.

Do you have areas in your life where you need clarity? Perhaps you aren't sure exactly what you believe about salvation, grace, the ordinances of the church, cultural trends, etc. Think about your life and see if anything comes to mind that may need to be clarified by the wisdom and teaching of the Holy Spirit.

_____

Do you have questions with which you need help? Do not be afraid to seek mature wise counsel from an older Christian. Make sure they are willing to search the scripture and pray with you for clarity on these issues.

4. Contamination can make the water unhealthy instead of "living".

Is your life contaminated by worldly thinking? _____

Worldly thinking can sneak in almost without notice. Fashion trends, changes in the music culture, media philosophies and lifestyles can influence your thinking to the point that these ideologies can become stronger than your spiritual beliefs. Humanistic beliefs are a threat to a growing Christian. You must learn to commit all your thinking and living to the presence of God in order that you will not lack spiritual power because you have embraced worldly thinking. What do you believe about sin? What would you consider unacceptable behavior? Where do you draw the line in dress and actions?

Write your thoughts on contamination. _____

_____

If you truly want to become a woman who is able to make commitments and stand by them:

1. Seek the Lord daily.
2. Ask for clarity on any questionable issue.
3. Search the scripture for wisdom (wisdom is the study next week).
4. Trust the Lord with your decisions.
5. Expand your commitment level by holding yourself accountable.
6. Seek a wise Christ-centered individual to be your encourager.
7. Expose areas that may be hindering you from becoming a fountain.
8. Have faith in God's ability to continue working in your life.
9. Ask for opportunities to share how God is working in your life.
10. When you fail, confess and move forward. Do not look back.

A prayer to end your week: Oh Lord, let me sense Your strength and power. Let me know that You are with me moment by moment and that You will guide me and fill me with wisdom to help make life more clear. Let me see things as You do and expand my heart to include Your love for others so that I might be a fountain of living water.

Thank You, Lord!

Your Thoughts:

_____

_____

_____

_____

_____

_____

_____

_____

_____

_____

_____

Becoming

a

Woman of Worth

WEEK # 3

WISE

BECOMING A WOMAN OF WORTH

WISE

MEMORY VERSE

I Timothy 4:12

"Let no man despise your youth, but be an example to the believers in word, in conduct, in love, in spirit, in faith, in purity."

Week # 3 - **Queen Esther** - Lesson #1

Principle: Wisdom is the result of total trust in God.

In becoming a **Woman of Worth** you will learn the difference between knowledge and wisdom.

Esther is the perfect example of a young woman who matured rapidly into a woman of wisdom and decision.

Knowledge is defined as "the attaining of information acquired through experience, practical ability or skill". Wisdom is defined as "the power of true and right discernment". Knowledge is information; wisdom is inspiration. We live in the most information rich generation ever known to man. Books. Media. The World Wide Web. All these sources can give knowledge. Wisdom, however, comes from only one source.

Read **Proverbs 2: 1-9** for the source of wisdom. Write down each reference to the attaining of wisdom given in these verses._____

_____

_____

_____

_____

The book of Esther is unique in that it does not directly mention God. Throughout the book there are numerous references to faith, obedience and the call for support and counsel to gain wisdom in making decisions. This makes it apparent that Mordecai and Esther depended on God. Indeed God did see them through the time of personal and national crisis.

How does one become wise? How old do you have to be to be wise? Can a young person have wisdom beyond their years?

Read **I Timothy 4:12** and write your comments_____

_____

_____

Esther's decision might not only alter her life, but could have an effect on the lives of her people, the Israelites. For background reading you will want to read the entire book of Esther.

The Providence of God

Without the providence of God, how could a young Jewish girl become the Queen of the Persian Empire? Do you believe in the providence of God?

_____

I. **Wisdom gained from family influence** - Esther 2:10-11 - Mordecai, an official in the palace of the royal family of Shushan in Persia was one of many Jews who remained behind after their captivity. His position of prominence at the Palace of Shushan exposed him to the happenings in the royal courts and the plots and plans to overthrow the king and eventually rid the kingdom of the Jewish people.

How close is the relationship within your family? Would you seek and take the counsel and advice of a family member? _____

How did Esther know she could trust in the counsel of Mordecai? _____

_____

After the death of Esther's parents, she was adopted by her cousin. Mordecai raised her as his own child and provided an environment of love for God, respect for her heritage as an Israelite and respect for the family.

> **Romans 8:15** "For you did not receive the spirit of bondage again to fear, but you received the Spirit of adoption by whom we cry out, Abba, Father."

Adoption is a biblical concept with deep spiritual meaning. The principal of adoption is vital in understanding your relationship with God as your father and Jesus as your brother. The concept of being a joint heir with Christ influences your acceptance of ownership and thanksgiving.

Read **Romans 8:15 -17** and write your comments regarding the concept of adoption._____

_____

_____

II. **Wisdom from personal observation - Esther 2:15** - Esther grew up observing Mordecai and how he went about making decisions. Because of his example, she was able to trust in his judgment. She also used her year of preparation to observe and listen to those around her. Wisdom comes from the ability to convert information into wisdom.

After the refusal of Vashti, the present Queen of Persia, the decree was given to search the land for "all the beautiful young virgins" in order to find a new Queen to replace Vashti. After the virgins were prepared, which included six months of oil and myrrh treatment and six months of perfumed treatment, they would be allowed one audience with the King after which he would decide who would become his new queen. Esther was gathered along with all the other young virgins. Due to observing the life of Mordecai, Esther was able to trust him and accept his counsel.

Your comments on why Vashti refused the King's command? _____

_____

During the twelve months that she was being prepared, she had much time to gain wisdom from those assigned as personal assistants. Hegai, being the custodian of the women, was in a position to give Esther much advice and counsel regarding the likes and dislikes of the king.

> **Esther 2:15** "she requested nothing but what Hegai the king's eunuch, the custodian of the woman advised."

Read **Esther 2:20** and write your comments. What qualities must Esther have possessed to be able to gain the favor of Hegai and "all who saw her"? Are these qualities genetic or can they be developed? _____

_____

The Plan of God

Four rapid events set the course for the rest of the book of Esther.

1. **Esther 2:17** - King Ahasuerus selects Esther as Queen of Persia.
2. **Esther 2:21-23** - After uncovering a plot to murder the king and informing Esther, Mordecai gains notoriety with the king.
3. **Esther 3:1-6** - King Ahasuerus promotes Haman. Haman becomes filled with pride, arrogance and jealousy.
4. **Esther 3:8-9** - Because of the jealousy of Haman against Mordecai, Haman orders a degree to destroy the Jews.

As the scripture unfolds, it becomes clear that one decision can make the difference in who God uses to fulfill His will. Esther and Mordecai are faced with vital decisions.

Read **Esther 4:14-17** - Comment on Mordecai's statement and Esther's request for a community fast. How important was the fast to Esther's decision?

> **A prayer for you:** Lord give me wisdom to know You, Your Word and Your Will.

III. **Wisdom from other sources - Esther 4:16** - What did Esther expect to gain from the support of her fellow Jews? How should outside advice influence your decisions? _____

Read **Proverbs 3:5-6** and write your comments regarding the steps in making wise decisions._____

_____

_____

Esther needed not only wisdom, but clarity in sorting out the facts before exposing Haman's plan to kill the Jews. The three days of fasting allowed her time to consider all the options and the best method of revealing the evil nature of Haman.

Esther 5:1-8 - The decision to have a feast for the King and Haman gave Esther the opportunity to show the King her affection. Haman was impressed to have been invited and after bragging to his wife, he was convinced that he held a favored spot with Esther and the King.

Read **Esther 5:9-14** - Write your comments regarding jealousy. What part do the emotions of jealousy, pride and deceit have in the character of Haman?

_____

_____

_____

Is there a difference between healthy and unhealthy jealousy? _____

Exodus 20:5 "You shall not bow down to them nor serve them. For I, the Lord your God, am a jealous God."

Esther 5:9-6:14 - Haman's wife and friends fed his selfish motives and jealous behavior. Haman sets his course for destruction by taking the bad advice of family and friends.

Write your comments regarding Haman's decision making process. _____

_____

Esther 7:1-10 - As Esther begins to reveal her petition to the King, she does so in dignity, submission and humility; yet with boldness. This reveals the depth of wisdom which was developed in Esther.

The true reason for the bad behavior of Haman is revealed by King Ahasuerus statement, "Who is he, and where is he, who would dare presume in his heart to do such a thing?"

The Provision of God

> **Matthew 15:18** "But those things which proceed out of the mouth come from the heart, and they defile a man."

Throughout the Old Testament it is recorded how God provided for the protection of the Jews. No one knows why God selected this nation to be His chosen people. However, it is clear that because of the provision of God, His people are spared from destruction. He always provides a way for His children to escape destruction.

Think over historical events which have been for the purpose of destroying the nation of Israel. Write your thoughts on these plans and how God provided for the safety of His people. Has there been a time when you were protected in a special way by God? _____

_____

_____

Why are the qualities of humility and submission significant to wisdom?

_____

_____

> **James 4:10** "Humble yourselves in the sight of the Lord, and He will lift you up."

Read **Esther 8-10** and comment on the following:

How did Esther's wisdom affect her cousin? _____

_____

How did Esther's wisdom affect her people? _____

_____

How did Esther's wisdom affect her relationship with King Ahasuerus?

_____

_____

Why did Esther show no mercy on the sons of Haman? _____

_____

How are the Jewish people continuing to be affected by the wisdom of Esther?

_____

_____

Close your day preparing for your day of fasting. Write your concerns.

PRAYING GOD'S WILL - Can I Know His Will for My Life?

God always hears our prayers, but we can expect results if we pray "in His will".

> I **John 5:14** "Now this is the confidence that we have in Him, that if we ask anything according to His will, He hears us."

Often the question is asked, "Can you know the will of God?"

God has told us some specific areas of His will which are general to every person. This is called His **specific will.** These are the areas where He has clearly stated... "this is My will...".

There is also God's **directive will,** individualized for each of His children. This is His will for your unique and special life.

As you study God's word, you will find what He says about His Will. Then as you obey what He has clearly defined, you will have increased wisdom to make decisions in areas which are not so clear.

The key to knowing God's will is obedience.

If you are obediently and faithfully seeking His will in what He has revealed through His Word, then does it not seem more likely that you will be able to discern what He desires for the obscure areas of your life?

There are four scriptures which state God's **specific will** for His children.

Read II Peter 3:9. Write this verse and your comment. _____

_____

When you pray for the salvation of the lost, you are praying God's **specific will** for their life.

Read **John 14:6-7.** Write your comments._____

_____

Your first prayer concern should always be salvation.

Ways to pray for the lost:

1. Pray by name that the person will know they have a need for salvation.
2. Pray that the person will be open to the Holy Spirit as He draws them to Himself.
3. Pray that the person will be daily reminded of God's love through events in their day.
4. Pray that Christian individuals will be placed in the person's life on a daily basis.
5. Pray that you will be usuable and available as a witness in their life.

Now that you know that salvation is God's **specific will** for every person, how is this information going to change the way you pray?

Will every individual be saved? What are your reasons for believing in this way?

_____

_____

The answer to many of the issues of life can be traced back to the fact that the person does not have an intimate relationship with God. They are trying to seek answers from someone they do not know very well.

Some people believe there is a God, respect God and admire God but do not **know** God. Think about the difference between having a knowledge of who God is and **knowing** God on an intimate basis.

Record in your journal the names of individuals who need an intimate relationship with God. Pray now for them!

Observations Regarding Wisdom

I. You will not necessarily have more wisdom as you grow older.
    A. Esther gained wisdom because she was teachable.
    B. Esther gained wisdom because she was receptive.

II. Wisdom can be gained by advice from wise family members.
    A. Esther took the advice of Mordecai.
    B. Esther's wise observations were crucial in making decisions.

III. Wisdom can be gained by surrounding yourself with wise counsel.
    A. Esther took the advice of Hegai.
    B. Esther gained wisdom from the examples of godly ancestors.

IV. Pride can stand in the way of attaining wisdom.
    A. Esther did not let the complements and accolades of those around her become a source of pride to keep her from acting in wise ways.
    B. Haman allowed pride to become one of his major problems and it was his downfall.

V. Humility is important in the gaining of wisdom.
    A. Esther continued to be humble and submissive.
    B. Humility was one reason Esther gained favor.

VI. Wisdom can be gained from surrounding yourself with prayer support.
    A. Esther called for support in prayer and fasting.
    B. Asking for wisdom is necessary to increasing wisdom.

VII. A wise person will not be jealous of others.
    A. Esther did not display actions which would keep her from being wise.
    B. Haman was consumed with jealousy toward Mordecai.

VII. Wisdom only comes from the ability to seek God and trust in His direction.
    A. Because of Esther's wise decisions, the children of Israel were spared from annihilation.
    B. The feast of Purim is celebrated because of the wise actions of Esther.

Review the life of Esther and write your comments regarding impressions of Esther and her wise actions. _____

_____

_____

Compare the actions of Vashti and the actions of Esther to see the contrast of behavior. _____

_____

_____

Write your comments regarding the behavior of Hegai. _____

_____

_____

Write your thoughts regarding the personality of Mordecai. _____

_____

_____

Why do you think that God is not mentioned by name in the book of Esther? __

_____

_____

What one thing impressed you about the life of Esther? _____

_____

Personal Applications - Wisdom

To become a **Woman of Worth** you must act in wise ways which display wisdom. You must have a desire to know God more intimately and to understand His wisdom. You must seek His Word to strengthen your maturity and understanding of human actions in contrast with spiritual wisdom. Human actions are based on selfish motives. Spiritual wisdom is based on the belief in the presence of God in your life through the power of the Holy Spirit and the faith that He will guide you in maturity and wisdom. You must ask for wisdom. An evaluation of personal actions can reveal how wise you are.

Esther reveals a woman who was teachable, and useable.

Are you teachable and useable? _____

God wants available people to fulfill His will for individuals and nations.

Has God ever called you to be an influence in the life of another person? How did you react to this? _____

_____

God gives wisdom to those who :

Respect His authority
Are humble
Submissive to His leading
Available to be used
Have a teachable spirit
Are courageous and strong
Ask for wisdom with the right motives

Wisdom is not to be equated with knowledge. Wisdom is a spiritual process bestowed by God on individuals who have a desire to grow in wisdom.

What recent decisions have you made? Did you ask for wisdom in making these decisions? _____

_____

_____

What process do you use in making decisions? _____

_____

The process to becoming a woman of wisdom:
1. Ask
2. Study about wisdom from God's word.
3. Seek God's answers before seeking any other opinion.

Now that you have studied the life of Esther, have you changed your concept of wisdom? Write your comment _____

_____

Scripture regarding wisdom

Genesis 24:12-58 - It takes wisdom to be submissive and sensitive to God
Exodus 2:1-10 - It takes wisdom to trust in God's ability to rescue
I Samuel 25:32-34 - It takes wisdom to be available to be used in unusual ways
Ruth 1:12-18 - It takes wisdom to follow God faithfully
Nehemiah 8:5-6 - It takes wisdom to know of God's holiness
Proverbs 3:21-26 - It takes wisdom to discern between right and wrong
Daniel 9:3-9 - It takes wisdom to understand God's righteousness and mercy
John 3:16 - It takes wisdom to believe in salvation through belief in Jesus
John 8:31-36 - It takes wisdom to understand the truth of Jesus and His love
James 1:5 - To have wisdom, you must ask for it

Spend time and write a prayer of thanksgiving for wisdom.

Thank God for giving you His Word.

Thank God for giving you His Spirit.

Thank God when you make wise decisions.

Proverbs 1:16 "How much better it is to get wisdom than gold! And to get understanding is to be chosen rather than silver."

As you seek God in becoming a **Woman of Worth** you should begin to have a new appreciation for the power of God in your life. You should sense your confidence rising and your self esteem reaching new levels. As your respect for God grows, your wisdom will also mature.

Proverbs 4:7-9 "Wisdom is the principal thing; Therefore get wisdom. And in all your getting, get understanding. Exalt her, and she will promote you; She will bring you honor, when you embrace her. She will place on your head an ornament of grace; A crown of glory she will deliver to you."

54

A prayer to end the week: Oh Lord, show me how to be wise according to Your wisdom. Reveal to me where I am not wise and forgive me when I do not seek Your counsel. Teach me according to Your word that I might be a blessing to others because of what You are doing in my life.

You are Holy, Lord!

Becoming
a
Woman of Worth

WEEK # 4

SUBMISSIVE

BECOMING A WOMAN OF WORTH

SUBMISSIVE

MEMORY VERSE
John 14:21
"He who has My commandments and keeps them, it is he who loves Me, and he who loves Me will be loved by My Father and I will love him and manifest Myself to him."

Week # 4 - **Mary Magdalene** - Lesson #1

Principle: To be loved by God, we must be submissive to the commandments of His son, Jesus.

To become a **Woman of Worth** you must be willing to learn what Jesus said and then be willing to obey His teachings. In doing so, you will find a stable foundation which is the cornerstone of a relationship with God.

Becoming a submissive woman requires obedience to the authority of Christ.

Submission has a negative definition in the vocabulary of many women in our society, however, submission is a positive biblical word. To be submissive under the authority of a Holy God, who not only created the universe, but created you, is essential to knowing Him on an intimate level. Submission is defined as "the act of yielding to the power, will, or authority of another". Other words for submission are obedience, surrender, acquiesce. The term acquiesce means "to quietly surrender or consent".

Most of us want our way and our first priority is to please ourselves in any given situation. As a Christian woman, it can be difficult to define submission because of the conflicting ideas demonstrated in our ego driven society. Consent and surrender sound like terms used in battle rather than terms used to define a loving caring relationship.

This week you will study what the Bible says about submission and what submission means to becoming a **Woman of Worth**.

Jesus gives the perfect picture of submission as He surrenders to the will of His Father. As Jesus surrendered to the nature of God, it strengthened Him to know and do God's will. His submission enabled Jesus to draw from God's power. This power is available to anyone who is willing to seek God and submit to His authority. This Jesus did in His humanity as an example for your life. Likewise, in yielding to the authority of God you will become stronger and more confident. You will grow in your understanding of the meaning of submission.

When submission turns sour, a dangerous situation can develop. A stronger individual can lord over a weaker, less confident person demanding that they submit. They might use such statements as, "I know better than you", "I am stronger than you", or "You must do as I say because God says so". In this situation there are two problems; one person who has a need to control and the other who isn't strong enough to resist the demands. This is a form of emotional abuse and often professional counseling is needed.

What is your understanding of submission?_____

_____

What do the terms, yield and surrender mean to you?_____

_____

Do you think that Jesus was a strong individual? _____

_____

How could Jesus have been the authority, yet been submitted to the authority of God? _____

_____

One quality of a **Woman of Worth** is the ability to recognize that God is the authority in everything and He will help you develop healthy relationships.

During Jesus' three years of ministry, He touched the hearts and lives of many individuals. One of these people was Mary Magdalene who ministered to Jesus and the disciples. She supported the spread of the gospel with her time and resources. Many women were involved in the ministry of Jesus.

Read **Luke 8:1-3** and write your thoughts. _____

_____

_____

I. **Submission to Jesus as the Great Physician**

Mary Magdalene was from the village of Magdala located about three miles from Capernaum along the Sea of Galilee. This town was known for its dye works and textile industries, but also had the unsavory reputation of harlotry and sexual indiscretions. There is no indication that Mary of Magdala was a prostitute, as is sometimes suggested. Since she was from a town with a bad reputation, had financial resources, and had no husband or family, it does leave some question as to her background. As you study the life of Mary, you will find that she was willing to submit by faith to the authority of Jesus and became a vital part of His life, ministry and message.

The scripture says she was filled with seven demons. What do you think may have been some of her problems? _____

_____

The number seven is used in scripture to represent "complete". Mary was totally consumed by evil and was under the control of evil spirits and physical infirmities brought on by this control.

Read **Proverbs 6:16-19** and list seven things that God hates. _____

_____

_____

59

It is certain that Jesus' message was a welcome relief for the disturbed Mary. Her health issues had made her life miserable. Her mental and emotional condition made her future bleak. She was suffering in an existence of bondage to Satan and blinded by darkness of mental illness.

> **John 8:12** "I am the light of the world. He who follows Me shall not walk in darkness, but have the light of life."

How do you think Mary responded to Jesus' statement, "I am the light of the world"? _____

_____

> **John 10:7** "I am the door, If anyone enters by Me, he will be saved, and will go in and out and find pasture."

How do you think Mary responded when she heard Jesus say, "I am the door."?

_____

_____

II. Submission to Jesus as Savior

When Mary Magdalene met Jesus, her life was transformed. She submitted to the healing power of Jesus and received His gift of salvation and eternal life. Then she became involved in the ministry of Jesus and spreading the message that had so changed her life. Because of her faith, she received hope, salvation, abundant life, and promise of eternal life to come. As she listened to His teachings, watched His life and saw the miracles of His works, she experienced the fullness of what Jesus meant when He spoke of abundant life. She was a **Woman of Worth**.

Read **John 10:10**. Write your thoughts. _____

_____

She knew Satan was a thief and had stolen her love of life and destroyed her mental and emotional health. Because of her relationship with Jesus Christ, she was restored. As you close this day, thank Jesus for your salvation.

When Mary submitted to Jesus' offer of healing, her life was altered for eternity. Her obedience and service were the evidence of the change in her life. There will be evidence of a change in the life of anyone who believes in Christ.

Read the following verses and see what Jesus asks of His followers.

Matthew 5: 43-44 _____

Matthew 7:1-6 _____

Matthew 10: 32-33 _____

Matthew 16: 24 _____

Matthew 28:19-20 _____

III. Submission to Jesus as Minister

Mary and several other women were willing to be available to serve Jesus and the disciples as they went about in ministry. These women gave of their substance (**Luke 8:3**) to meet the expenses of the traveling evangelists.

Being married to a full time vocational evangelist, I know how important it is to have people who are available to serve and support the ministry. These women played a vital part in allowing Jesus and the disciples freedom to do their work without having to think about food and finances.

Submission is often displayed through a willingness to serve and encourage. Submitting to the authority of Christ takes strength and determination.

IV. Submission to Jesus as Redeemer

Mary was not only obedient, but faithful to Jesus.

Read **Mark 15:40-41**; **Matthew 27:55-61**; **John 19:25**. What are your comments regarding the faithfulness of Mary.

_____

_____

_____

As Mary stood by the cross, the memories of the past three years of her life must have moved through her mind. She watched Jesus minister to children, feed thousands, touch the lame and blind and raise the dead. The greatest evidence to Mary Magdalene of Jesus' power was in her own life and how her life was changed after she met Jesus. She knew first hand His power and authority. She saw the intimate relationship that He had with God, His father.

At the cross, what questions do you think Mary may have had? _____

_____

_____

How would she have interacted with the other followers of Jesus?_____

_____

_____

Do you think Mary knew at the time of Jesus' crucifixion that He was the Savior of the world?_____

_____

V. Submission to Jesus as Resurrection and Life

Read **Matthew 28:1**; **Mark 16: 1-10**; **John 20:11** and comment on these events. _____

_____

_____

How must Mary have felt when she found the tomb empty? _____

_____

VI. Submission to Jesus as Messenger of Eternal Life

Mary most certainly was healed, or else she could not have watched the mistreatment, trial, judgement, death and burial of Jesus. Her faith in Christ was her source of strength to walk through those dark hours. Think of the sadness, hurt, anger, grief, confusion, and questions that her soul must have had. We do not see her waiver in her commitment to Jesus.

Read **Mark 16:1-8** and **John 20:1-18** and write your comments on Mary's reaction to the resurrection of Jesus. _____

_____

_____

Did Mary come expecting the tomb to be empty? _____

_____

Why was Mary weeping? _____

_____

Why did Mary not recognize Jesus? _____

_____

John 20: 15-16 Jesus said to her, "Woman, why are you weeping? Whom are you seeking?" She, supposing Him to be the gardener, said to Him, "Sir, if you have carried Him away, tell me where You have laid Him, and I will take Him away." Jesus said to her, "Mary!"

When Jesus called her name, "Mary", what emotions did she feel? _____

_____

End this day in prayer for the power of healing.

A POWERFUL PRAYER LIFE

> **Zechariah 4:5b-6** "...did you really fast for ME—for ME? When you eat and when you drink, do you not eat and drink for yourselves?"

Last week, as you fasted, you studied about God's will for every person. Just as God has revealed how you can know His will, He has also revealed some of the reasons why your prayer life seems powerless. Have you ever prayed and felt that your prayers were getting nowhere? Did God take a coffee break when you were praying? Maybe He was busy listening to someone else instead.

As you mature as a **Woman of Worth**, you will be glad to know that God is **always** available to you. You are so special that God wants to meet your needs. He wants your life to be filled to capacity with His presence, His power, and His love. He offers you His forgiveness, His mercy and His grace. All of these are yours as a benefit of your obedience.

If your prayer life has become stale and you do not sense a strength and power in your life, maybe a closer examination is needed.

I. Praying with selfish motives is one reason for a powerless prayer life.

Read **James 4:3** Write your comments regarding selfish motives.

_____

Can you identify any selfish (wrong) motives as you are praying? _____

_____

Are you praying your will and not God's will? Are you trying to manipulate God into meeting your requests? When you pray, are your prayers repetitive? Do you talk to God more about what you want or what He wants for you? Do you praise as you pray?

As you fast and pray today, consider selfishness and sin in your life.

Identify selfish motives in your prayer life. by asking these questions.

Do I believe God can answer prayer?
Why do I want this prayer answered?
Am I being obedient to the word of God?
Ask God to show me how to pray specifically.

> **John 14:3** "If anyone loves me, he will keep My word; and My Father will love him and We will come to him and make Our home with him."

II. Sinful behavior is another reason for a powerless prayer life.

Read **Psalm 66:18** and write your thoughts. _____

_____

Read **James 4:17** and write the definition of sin. _____

_____

Iniquity is another word for sin.   Sin comes in a multitude of colors and is often easier to identify in the lives of others. Is sin simply bad behavior? Sin is any disobedience against God. Have you ever sensed the leading of the Holy Spirit and chosen to ignore? That is sin. Have you refused to listen to the voice of the Spirit of God in your life? That is sin, too. Have you passed along a juicy bit of gossip? Sin? Yes. Were you too busy to obey when God pressed upon your heart to spend time witnessing? Oops! Sin. Sin can become a stronghold taking root between your spirit and your flesh.

Another definition of sin is **"missing the mark"**. Sin is not only committing a wrong act against God, it is omitting to obey His Word and spend time with Him.

My father in law, J.T. Drace, who retired after pastoring for over fifty years, would often say, "The problem with sin is 'I' am always in the middle".

My evangelist husband, Jerry Drace, says, "Sin takes you further than you want to go, keeps you longer than you want to stay, and costs more than you want to pay."

65

What would you place on your sin list? _____

Read **Exodus 20:1-17** and think about how you define sin.

1. Have I allowed anything to become more important than God? Family. Job. Money. Recreation. Friends. Church. Behaviors. Material things.

2. Have I allowed perversions into my mind? What types of movies do I watch? What type of music do I spend my money on? Is it honoring to God? What type of language do I use and allow used in my presence? Am I using my computer in the right ways?

3. How do I honor the sabbath? Do I shop on Sunday? Do I make excuses because I don't have any other time to go shopping? Do I take time to rest and enjoy family and friends on the sabbath? How regular am I in church attendance? Am I in Bible study regularly? Do I attempt to practice what I say I believe?

4. Do I honor my parents? How can honor be given to parents who are not believers? The first priority of a Christian is to honor God and by doing so, you are honoring others.

5. Can I commit murder without drawing a gun or wielding a weapon? Is gossip slander? What do I think about the life of the unborn and the elderly?

6. What is considered adulterous behavior?

7. What is stealing? Am I fair to my employer with my time? Do I cheat? Am I stealing time from those who love me to spend with people who do not bring out the best in me?

8. How would I define "to bear false witness"? Am I always truthful? Do I ever distort or twist the truth? Do I put others down in order to build myself up?

9. What is coveting? Do I work harder so that I can have more? How do I take care of my belongings? Am I grateful? Do I say thank you?

Sin can root into your life and become a stronghold (a wall between you and your intimacy with God). These types of sins have to be taken consistently before the Lord. Addictions are particularly hard to overcome because they can control over your entire life. If you have a situation like this, remember that the Lord is stronger than anything and by His strength, you can win over sin.

You can win over sin!

Tips on keeping your prayer life fresh and exciting.

Romans 3:23 - Admit that you are struggling with sin in your life.
I John 1:9 - Confess specific behaviors, attitudes or motives.
Psalm 51:15-17 - Repent and ask forgiveness.
Micah 7:19 - Accept that God can forgive you and will forget your sin.

Make a list of family and friends and commit to pray for them by name each day. Keep your list brief in order to focus on specific prayer needs. Many times our prayer list becomes so lengthy that we cannot spend enough prayer time on each request.

When you pray begin with praise to God for who He is.
Ask the Lord to reveal any selfish motive or sinful behavior.
Include thanksgiving in your prayer.
Now you are ready to ask your petitions.

Expect results when you confess sin. Know that God answers prayer in His time and sometimes answers to prayer come in minute ways rather than in large miraculous ways.

Be open with the Lord, He knows anyway and wants you to be able to experience Him in His fullness. He wants His power to fill up your life and spill out on those around you with grace and mercy.

If you fill up, you will spill out!

End this day with a prayer of gratitude for forgiveness. Tell God how excited you are about what He is going to do **in** and **through** you.

67

Observations Regarding Submission

Mary is mentioned in all four gospels in fourteen references. In eight of these references she is mentioned along with other women. Her name heads the list indicating her position of readiness to serve. The other five references are in regard to the death and resurrection of Jesus. Through the death of Jesus on the cross and the celebration of His resurrection, she is steadfast in her devotion.

1. Mary's changed life is an example of the miracle of salvation.

What evidence indicates that the life of Mary was completely altered and never returned to the state of total bondage under the control of Satan?

_____

_____

_____

Read **John 20:17-18** and answer the following?

What was the message given to Mary to deliver to the others? _____

_____

What did Jesus mean when He said, "I am ascending to My Father and your Father, and to My God and your God." _____

_____

Why do you think the message of Hope was given to Mary instead of Peter or John? _____

What do you think Mary must have felt to hear Jesus call her by name? _____

_____

2. Mary's changed life is reflected in her obedience and faith. Write the evidence of Mary's faithfulness and obedience.

_____

_____

> **Hebrews 11:6** "Without faith it is impossible to please Him, for he who comes to God must believe that He is, and that He is a rewarder of those who diligently seek Him."

It requires faith to believe, faith to trust and faith to continue to daily submit obediently to Jesus. What does it mean to diligently seek Jesus? _____

_____

3. Mary's changed life reveals God's truth and faithfulness through the power of Jesus. There is no need to return to the old way of life when Jesus offers the promise of abundant life and hope for eternity.

> **II Corinthians 5:17** "If anyone is in Christ, he/she is a new creation; old things have passed away; behold, all things have become new."

Why would Mary want to return to a life of mental sickness when she had experienced the complete healing of her mind, body and soul?

4. Mary's changed life results in the announcement of the resurrected Lord. She had the honor of telling Peter, the disciples and other believers that **"He is Risen"!**

Jesus ministry to Mary shows:

The status of women has been lifted to a position of value and importance.
God's plans are not dictated by culture.
There is a place for women in ministry.
Salvation through Jesus Christ is available to anyone.
God uses available people to spread the message of His love.

As you end this day, list why you think Mary was a **Woman of Worth.**

Personal Applications - Submission

Many references are made in the ministry of Jesus to both demonic possession and mental illness and how He healed people of these illnesses. Mental illness is an enormous problem in our culture. It has been reported by the American Medical Association that many hospital beds are occupied by people who have some sort of physical problem linked to illness in the mind and emotions.

Counselors are in great demand today. Many churches are employing full time counselors to help in dealing with the problems of emotional and mental illness. Medication can be received for the treatment of depression, anxiety, stress, grief, insomnia, and a wide variety of other problems. Some of these are legitimate medical problems; others are directly linked to problems of the mind. Inability to cope with death, loss, fear, anger, self esteem, rejection, stress and guilt can lead to a path of mental illness. When a person becomes emotionally and mentally sick, a perfect environment is created for Satan to set up residence.

How common is mental illness today? _____

Not all mental illness is demonic possession, but it is quite clear that Satan can **possess** the mind, body and spirit of any person without Christ. Satan can also **oppress** a child of God in order to render that person ineffective for the cause of Christ. Jesus has the power to heal, cleanse and keep your mind from Satanic control.

How would you define demonic influence?

_____

_____

What do you think is the difference between possession and oppression? _____

_____

Possession and oppression are very different. Mary was possessed and only deliverance through salvation in Christ could release her from the control of Satan. The Bible says that Jesus cast out demons.

The old saying, "An idle mind is the devil's workshop" is true.

1. A **non-believer** can be oppressed or possessed by Satan.
    Read the following examples and write your thoughts.
    Matthew 8:28-34 - (two possessed men)
    Mark 1:23-26 - (man with unclean spirit)
    Mark 5:1-20 - (man with legions of demons)

2. A **believer** cannot be possessed but can be oppressed by evil influences.
    Read **Matthew 26:69-75**. Peter's denial of Jesus is an example of how Satan oppresses. Peter was frightened and confused at the time of Jesus' arrest. Three times Peter denied he was a follower of Jesus. He cursed to emphasize that he didn't know Him. His spirit was in conflict of choices. "Do I truthfully admit to being a follower of Christ or do I lie?" Peter made his choice. How did Peter deal with the realization that he had failed? Have you ever denied Christ?

Temptation came, Satan oppressed, Peter submitted to Satan.

    Read Romans 6: 16; Romans 7:19-25. Paul explains spiritual warfare. He says what he wants to do he doesn't, and what he doesn't want to do he does. Submitting to temptation is a battle in the life of every believer. The choice is to submit to the Lordship of Christ or to submit to the oppression of Satan. Every person is free to make choices but not free to choose the consequences of their choices.

Examine your spiritual life. To whom do you most often submit? _____

When you are tempted, do you how know to respond to Satan's attempts to gain control over your life? _____

_____

    Read **I Corinthians 10:13** and write your thoughts. _____

_____

There is always a way of escape when faced with temptation!

Spiritual victory comes from daily submission to Jesus.

Steps of submission to the Lordship of Christ.

1. **John 10:28-30** - Belief and acceptance of Christ.
2. **John 15:10-11** - Obedience to His teachings.
3. **John 8:31-36** - Commitment to the Word of God.
4. **John 14:16-21** - Trust in the presence and power of the Holy Spirit.

I Corinthians 2:11 "For no other foundation can anyone lay than that which is laid, which is Jesus Christ."

Think about and pray about these statements.

Submission is a choice.
There is hope in Christ.
Peace of mind and heart come from a personal relationship with Jesus.
Strength for daily living comes from study of the scriptures.
Counseling is sometimes necessary to help in dealing with difficulty.
The power to face any situation is available to those who ask.

Ask these questions:

Am I submitting to any unholy behavior?
Do I feel overwhelmed by worldly influences?
Are the conditions of my life generating thoughts of doubt or despair?

A Woman of Worth must be prepared to battle temptation.

As you close this study on submission, prayerfully read **Ephesians 6:10-17** and make a list of the armor and what each piece represents in the battle for authority.

A Prayer to close your week: Oh Lord, Help me to know You, Your power and Your strength. Let me sense Your presence in my life all day so that I might have the assurance of Your wisdom. Help me to recognize Your authority and to willfully trust my life into Your hands. Make my heart strong so that I am ready to battle against the powers that rise against You. Show me how to submit to Your Word and to know and do Your will. Thank you for Your grace and mercy. You are all powerful and You are God. You, Oh Lord, are mighty!

Becoming
a
Woman of Worth

WEEK # 5

VICTORIOUS

BECOMING A WOMAN OF WORTH

VICTORIOUS

Week # 5 - **Hannah** - Lesson #1

Principle: Dealing with difficulty requires spiritual strength.

In learning about becoming a **Woman of Worth,** you will study several areas. One often asked question is, "How do I deal with stress?" Everyone has stress in their lives. The level of stress depends on what is going on in your life.

Knowing how to handle life's challenges is paramount in your becoming a **Woman of Worth.**

Usually when I am in the middle of a stressful situation, I can keep it in check by simply bringing it to the Lord and leaving it there. However, sometimes the stress level is almost overwhelming. What can you do about excess stress?

The breaking point may be just at the door of your life, pressing upon you with pressure that seems unbearable. Excess stress can lead to health problems, mental problems, and emotional problems.

Depression is one of the most common health problems relating to excess stress. Many drugs are available to aide in battling stress related depression. Suicide, as an escape from stress, is on the increase and is more common today than ever before. People are looking for ways to handle stress.

This week we will study how to have victory over stressful situations.

Hannah is a popular name. Many Sunday School classes have been named "the Hannah class". Hannah has been used as an example of faith, prayer, and dedication. However, as you look closely at the life of Hannah, you will see a woman who had to confront her bitterness, frustration, anger and depression **before** she became a woman of faith, prayer and dedication.

If you interviewed Hannah at the beginning of I Samuel 1, she would not voice self assurance or confidence in being a **Woman of Worth.** Her appearance would indicate an unhappy, oppressed woman and her attitude would reveal her emotional status.

Read **I Samuel 1:1-20** to see how Hannah was overwhelmed with stress and how her emotions were spiraling out of control. She was not being defeated because of the obstacles in her life, she was being defeated because of where she was spiritually. Can you relate?

I Samuel 1:2
....."and he had two wives, the name of one was Hannah and the name of the other was Peninnah."

1. **Captured by culture**. What comment can you make regarding the cultural environment of Elkanah, Hannah and Peninnah?_____

_____

Education, medicine, economy, family, etc. are all influenced by the trends of society. The time period just before the life of Hannah is indicative of the cultural environment.

Read **Judges 21: 25** for a revealing picture of the cultural environment in which Hannah lived. Write your comments. _____

_____

History records the influence of cultural trends on every society.

Exodus 14: 12 "Is this not the word that we told you in Egypt, saying, 'Let us alone that we may serve the Egyptians?' For it would have been better for us to serve the Egyptians than that we should die in the wilderness."

After spending 430 years in captivity in Egypt, the Israelites had become captivated by the Egyptian culture. Ideologies, philosophies, values, fashion trends, behaviors, ethics, and religious practices all come under the captivity of the culture in which you live.

Read **Exodus 14: 12 and 16:3** and write your comments regarding the influence the Egyptian culture had on the Israelites. _____

_____

2. **Madness in their marriage.** Another difficulty in the life of Hannah was caused by the embracing of polygamy. By having two wives, Elkanah found himself in a marriage environment influenced by a vengeful, meanspirited wife, Peninnah, who oppressed his other wife, Hannah.

Read **I Samuel 1: 2-5.** The friction between the women is obvious. What do you see as causing the friction in this home? _____

_____

_____

3. **Physical problems.** Hannah was faced with another societal problem in that she had no children. It was the ultimate fulfillment of a woman to have a male child and Hannah was filled with grief in the fact that she was barren.

Read **I Samuel 1:5-6.** Write your comments regarding the statement "and God closed her womb". _____

_____

_____

Could it be that God had closed her womb because she was not spiritually ready to handle the responsibility of being the mother of Samuel? _____

> **Genesis 20:17-18** "So Abraham prayed to God; and God healed Abimelech, his wife, and his maidservants. Then they bore children, for the Lord had closed up all the wombs of the house of Abimelech because of Sarah, Abraham's wife."

4. **Ruined relationship.** How hard would it be to live with constant bickering in your home? Peninnah is the perfect picture of a nemesis. She was mean, conniving, and hateful. Can't you sense the disdain in Peninnah?

Read **I Samuel 1:6**. Write your description of Peninnah and her treatment of Hannah? How do you think she spoke to her children regarding Hannah?

_____

_____

Whenever we begin to take on the atmosphere of our surrounding culture, there will be problems. Acceptance and tolerance of bad behavior can cause deep emotional barriers.

5. **Emotional instability.** - It is easy to allow the difficulties in life to bring chaos to our emotional and mental stability. Depression can become a stronghold and anger can easily grow into bitterness. Hannah was an emotional mess. She had begun a spiral into the pit of self centeredness and self pity. When a person allows their problems to take control of their life, then their life is out of control.

Read **I Samuel 1:6-9**. Write your description of the emotional state of Hannah. _____

_____

6. **Spiritually shattered.** Hannah did not have a religious problem. Her family was very obedient to the religious practices of the Jewish faith. Temple worship regularly, sacrifices according to the law, offerings and tithes (even a double portion) were part of their religious habits.

Read **I Samuel 1:3-4**. Describe why religious practices did not satisfy Hannah. _____

End your study time today by reviewing what you believe about being religious in contrast to being spiritual.

Hannah presents a picture of a depressed, stress-filled, heartbroken woman who was faithful in her religious practices. It was not her religious disciplines that helped her overcome her difficulty.

Read **I Samuel 1:11-12.** Write your thoughts on how to live in victory.

_____

_____

Elkanah, Hannah's husband could not solve her problem. He loved her and tried to assure her of his love by giving her extra portions of offering for worship. Money wasn't the answer to her problem. Likewise, Eli could not solve Hannah's problem. He made an error in his observation of Hannah's prayers. How did Hannah respond?

I. **Presented the problem to the right person. I Samuel 1:11** _____

I Samuel 1:11	
"She said, "Oh Lord of hosts, if you will indeed look on the affliction of your maidservant and remember me, and not forget your maidservant, but will give your maidservant a male child, then I will give him to the Lord all the days of his life..."	_____ Hannah cried out to God, **"O Lord of Hosts"**. The definition of maidservant is "a female servant". Would you consider the position of maidservant to be negative or positive? _____ _____ Read **John 13:13-15** for Jesus description of servanthood. Five times Hannah refers to herself as **maidservant"**.

She is stating her willingness to submit to the authority of God. The spiritual description of a servant is one who is willing to serve with an attitude of thanksgiving, love and obedience. A servant attitude with a servant's heart is the beginning of the transformation of Hannah from a depressed, bitter, frustrated woman into a joy-filled, content **Woman of Worth.**

2. **Position with the right attitude.** Hannah's attitude toward life was a significant reason for her difficulty. She couldn't see beyond her depression. As she wept, did not eat, and was miserable, she began to spiral into despair. She allowed her personal problems to overwhelm her. Her weakened faith would not allow her to trust God and to trust in the power of prayer.

Reread **I Samuel 1:11.** Write your thoughts on Hannah's attitude toward herself and her faith in God's ability to hear her prayers. _____

_____

3. **Prayer with the right motive**. Hannah needed to come to terms with her own prayer request. Why did she want a baby? Was it only to satisfy her need to become a mother or was there a greater reason? Was she trying to one-up Peninnah? Did she have any idea that her firstborn would be Samuel? Write your thoughts on these questions.

> **Hebrews 11:6**
>
> "Without faith it is impossible to please Him, for he who comes to God must believe that He is, and that He is a rewarder of those who diligently seek Him."

_____

Read **I Samuel 1:12-16** What four words indicate the change that was taking place in Hannah?

_____

a. **I Samuel 1:12** - "continued" - She did not stop praying until she experienced relief in her spirit.
b. **I Samuel 1:13** - "heart" - She went to the core of her problem. It was a heart problem.
c. **I Samuel 1:15** - "poured" - She did not hold back anything from God.
d. **I Samuel 1: 16** - "abundance" - She exposed herself totally to the power of God which allowed Him to begin to work in her life.

4. **Personal purification is vital to prayer.** Hannah could not come to a place of release until she admitted and confronted her part in her problems. "Out of the abundance of my complaint and grief I have spoken until now". When Hannah was able to completely open up to God from the root of the problem, then God began to immediately work in her life. She could sense the relief and peace as she trusted God.

Write your thoughts on how these four words can change your prayer life._____

_____

_____

Once Hannah was able to call on God with a renewed faith and place herself under His authority, it enabled her to pray with the right motive. As Hannah recognized her dependence on God and began to rest in God's sovereignty, then the transformation of her life began.

5. **Place problems faithfully in God's care** - Read **I Samuel 1:18.** Write your thoughts on the proof of the change in Hannah's attitude about her problems.

_____

_____

_____

Do you think Elkanah and Peninnah were aware of the change in Hannah?

Read **I Samuel I:19** Do you think worship was more meaningful for Hannah after this experience? _____

_____

6. **Patiently waited on God to work** - Hannah ended her prayer time renewed in every way, physically, emotionally, and spiritually. Did she have an immediate answer to her prayer request? How did she know that God was working in her life? Write your comments._____

_____

I Samuel 1:20 "In the process of time, Hannah conceived and bore a son, and called his name Samuel, saying, 'because I have asked for him from the Lord.'"

The proof of a changed life is in the **fruit** of a changed life. Hannah was changed. Her countenance, her attitude and her spiritual maturity are all indications that she indeed experienced victory over her problems.

7. **Praise with a joyful heart.** Read **I Samuel 1:26 - 2:2.** Write your thoughts on the proof of the victory that Hannah experienced. _____

_____

_____

_____

_____

One proof of the dimension of Hannah's victory can be found in **I Samuel 2:1** "I smile at my enemies". Who had been her enemy? There will always be results from a transformed life.

Did Hannah follow through with her vow regarding her son?

Refer to your thoughts regarding the scripture which says "and God closed her womb". Read **I Samuel 2:21** for a tangible result of the victory that Hannah experienced. How many children did Hannah have? _____

Samuel was used of God to guide a nation. Not only was Hannah obedient and faithful to God with her vow but as she followed through, she was an example of obedience and faithfulness to Samuel. Samuel's willingness to be used of God resulted in the anointing of two kings, Saul and David. The record of the life of Samuel continues to be an inspiration of obedience and faith.

> **I Samuel 3:19-20 -** "So Samuel grew, and the Lord was with him and let none of his words fall to the ground. All Israel from Dan to Beersheba knew that Samuel had been established as a prophet of the Lord."

End your study time today with a prayer of praise. Write your prayer.

A THANKFUL HEART

Have you ever heard this statement? "I wish I knew the will of God."

God has told us several things which **are** His will. Salvation for every person is the very heart of God. His love not only provided salvation for you through Jesus but as you come to know Him, He tells you how to have a life filled with His goodness and glory. He wants you to be victorious **through** any situation.

Read **I Thessalonians 5:16-18.** Write three statements which give a clear word from God regarding His will for your life. _____

_____

_____

_____

I. **Rejoice always!** Begin each day with an exclamation of worship.

Read **Psalm 95: 1-7.** Make a list of reasons you should be filled with joy. Carry this list with you today and throughout the day read over the list and repeat back to God what this means to you. When your day turns sour, look to the Lord to renew you and take in a deep breath of His presence. Ask and you will receive. His Holy Spirit will restore your joy.

I Thessalonians 5:16-18
"Rejoice always, pray without ceasing, in everything give thanks; for this is the will of God in Christ Jesus for you."

Place your mind under the control of the Holy Spirit. Ask Him to fill you with worship today.

II. Pray without ceasing!

How can you pray without ceasing when you are busy with family, job and many other things which demand your attention and time?

Tomorrow try this excercise. Pray for each person that you encounter. Whether family, friend, co-worker, fellow student, or stranger; offer a prayer for their life. At the end of the day record your thoughts on this activity.

Remember it is God's will that you be in a continual attitude of prayer. It is through prayer that we gain access to the intimate relationship which allows us to truly experience life in the power of God.

III. Give thanks in all things!

There are sicknesses, financial problems, family issues, and problems in my church. God wants me to have a thankful heart in all this? Is it truly possible to have a thankful heart all the time?

Read **I Thessalonians 5:18**. Write the verse. _____

_____

_____

Did Jesus have to deal with daily frustrations? How did he maintain such a close relationship with God? Did Jesus always live His life as an example of how we should be living our lives?

Read **Mark 1:35**. Write your thoughts._____

_____

Luke 5:16 "So He Himself often withdrew into the wilderness and prayed."

If you truly want to be centered in God's will, then you will need to take time to analyze your attitudes and emotions under the microscope of God's **specific will**.

What is the most difficult situation you have recently faced? How did you react? How should you have reacted? _____

_____

What are you doing to insure that you will be in a continual state of prayer? _____

_____

Take the rest of your time to make a list of 10 things for which you are thankful and why you have placed these things on your list.

1. _____

2. _____

3. _____

4. _____

5. _____

6. _____

7. _____

8. _____

9. _____

10. _____

Observations Regarding Victory

Hannah is a wonderful example of a woman who was overwhelmed with stress and faced obstacles which may have seemed impossible to overcome. Often stress comes from only a few areas of life; but for Hannah, her life was consumed with difficulties. By her faith and out of her trust in a Holy God, we see how she was able to release **all** of her difficult situations. Out of her experience at Shiloh, she was able to patiently face each day with joy and praise.

Read again **I Samuel 1:1-20**.

1. How had society and culture become an obstacle for Hannah? _____

_____

_____

_____

2. Why do you think Peninnah disliked Hannah? _____

_____

3. Do you think that her attitude was a problem for her children and how might it have affected her relationship with Elkanah? _____

_____

_____

4. The fact that Hannah was a deeply religious person did not help her in facing the difficulties in her life. Why? _____

_____

_____

5. Is there a difference between being religious and having a personal relationship with God through Jesus Christ? How did Hannah learn of a loving caring God?

_____

_____

_____

6. How do you know that Hannah was emotionally ill? _____

_____

_____

7. Why do you think Eli observed Hannah in the way that he did? _____

_____

_____

8. Why was Hannah seemingly not offended by Eli's remarks? _____

_____

_____

9. What was Hannah's first step toward overcoming her obstacles? _____

_____

_____

10. How are we certain that Hannah had truly dealt with her difficult situation and obtained victory? _____

_____

11. Observe **I Samuel 1:7, 10**. Can you observe the contrast in Hannah's attitude toward worship? Write your thoughts. _____

_____

12. Did Hannah have an immediate answer to her request?_____

_____

How could she leave with such peace and confidence? _____

_____

12. The change in Hannah was obvious. How might this visible change have affected her relationship with Elkanah, Peninnah and the children? _____

_____

13. In releasing her difficult life to the Lord, she began to immediately experience the "fullness of life" spoken of by Jesus in **John 10:10**. There was an inner transformation which took place in Hannah which allowed her to trust God with her difficulties and was noticeable to others who knew her.

Some of her difficulties were gone, some altered and some did not change. She also had some new problems to face, however she was at peace.

How was her situation altered?
What about her situation was deleted?
What did not change about her situation?
What new difficulties did she face?

Often what is needed is not an immediate answer to your prayers but peace to endure and deal with the daily aggravations.

Release brings peace.

Personal Applications - Victory

The inability to handle difficult situations is one of the main reasons for stress and related health problems in our present culture. Eating disorders, sleep disorders, high blood pressure, headaches, stomach and intestinal problems, and depression are all symptomatic of stress. The prescription drug industry is making gazillions of dollars on drugs to help with stress related illness.

How do you handle difficulty? Do you withdraw, shop, pout, eat, whine, become angry, go to bed, take medications, cry? All of us have stress and life is filled with challenges any of which can bring about despondency, despair and depression. Seasons of discouragement are a normal part of life.

You need to often be reminded that one of Satan's main areas of attack in the "battle for your life" is to get you into a state of discouragement which will render you unable to trust God and cause you to be ineffective in sharing your love for Jesus.

I Peter 5:8 "Be sober, be vigilant; because your adversary, the devil, walks about like a roaring lion, seeking whom he may devour."

After observing the life of Hannah, can you relate to any of her frustrations?

_____

_____

_____

Hannah was pressured because of the traditions of her culture, how has the culture of today invaded your life and the life of your family? _____

_____

_____

Hannah had problems in her marriage brought on by relational stress. Many blended families deal with daily problems which are a result from strained relationships from former marriages.

What encouragement can be gained from Hannah to help with the challenges of remarriage? _____

_____

_____

What can be done to promote a peaceful relationship with ex-spouses? _____

_____

_____

_____

How can you help children deal with difficult relationships, anger and hurt?

_____

_____

Is anger ever appropriate? When does anger become sin? _____

_____

_____

Read **John 2:13-16**. Write your comments. _____

_____

Read **Psalm 4:4**. Write your comments. _____

_____

Peninnah provoked Hannah to tears "year by year". Have you ever experienced this type of brutality? _____

How did you deal with the situation? _____

Bitterness is the continuation of unresolved anger. What indications do you see that confirms Hannah was bitter? Is there unresolved anger in your life? How do you plan to handle anger or bitterness in the future? _____

_____

When you seek to make peace with a nemesis, does that insure a positive response? _____

What should you do when you know that your adversary is going to continue to "provoke" you? _____

_____

Are you willing to place this situation in God's care and leave it there? _____

Write a prayer of commitment regarding this person. _____

_____

> **I Samuel 2:1** "And Hannah prayed and said, 'My heart rejoices in the Lord; my horn is exalted in the Lord. I smile at my enemies, because I rejoice in Your salvation.'"

How can a smile release pent up anger? Read **Proverbs 15:13.** Write your comments. _____

_____

Read **Romans 12:20-21**. Write your comments._____

_____

Hannah sought the Lord from the depth of her soul. She was released from the bondage of hurt, despair, anger, bitterness, desperation, and depression. After Eli's first reaction, how did he become a source of affirmation and comfort?

_____

Who do you go to for confirmation, and encouragement? _____

_____

Read **Proverbs 25:19**. What caution should be taken when seeking advice and counsel? _____

_____

Sometimes a situation must become almost hopeless and desperate before help is sought. How can you be a source of help to someone who is in a situation similar to that of Hannah? _____

_____

How important to you is personal worship? How important is discipline to your consistency in maintaining a regular worship time? _____

How can you encourage other women to develop a daily time of personal worship?

_____

When Hannah "poured out" her soul before the Lord, it required her to bare all. Many times we hold back our pet problems because of personal pride, embarrassment, or refusal to admit to difficulty. Sometimes this may be due to a lack of belief that God cares and has the answer to the problem.
Can you trust God with **all** your challenges? _____

Write down some of your difficult areas ? _____

What is your plan in dealing with these areas? _____

If you trust God, act on faith and ask; you can be cleansed and empowered!

> **I Corinthians 15:57** - "Thanks be to God, who gives us the victory through our Lord Jesus Christ."

Meditate and pray about these statements.

1. Everything has a spiritual basis.

2. Desperate situations require faith, trust and obedience.

3. To have victory, you must first have faith and trust God. Once you exercise your faith, then victory will come through diligence and dedication.

4. Daily frustrations are to be expected.

5. There is a difference between righteous and unrighteous anger.

6. The **primary** source of confirmation from God will come from His word and your prayer time.

7. A word of encouragement from another Christian may become a **secondary** source of confirmation from God.

8. The deeper the despair, the greater the sense of release when it is finally given to the Lord.

9. Only through God can you experience victory over difficulty.

10. Review the seven steps from this lesson on how to become a victorious **Woman of Worth.**

> **A prayer to end your week:** Oh Lord, You are Holy. Thank You for helping me today. Show me where I am not trusting You. I give You everything in my life. You alone are my strength and comfort. Help me to faithfully and obediently trust You to help me become victorious in all things. Oh Lord, You are Holy!
>
> Holy, Holy, Holy is the Lord!

Your Thoughts:

Becoming
a
Woman of Worth

WEEK # 6

DEVOTED

BECOMING A WOMAN OF WORTH

DEVOTED

MEMORY VERSE

I Corinthians 12: 4-6

"Now there are diversities of gifts, but the same Spirit. There are differences of ministries, but the same Lord and there are diversities of activites, but it is the same God who works all in all."

Week # 6 - **Martha and Mary** - Lesson #1

Principle: Devotion develops desire!

To become a **Woman of Worth** you must develop a heart devoted to the Lord. Out of a devoted heart will develop a desire to serve the Lord and from that desire will come the revelation of your spiritual gifts and direction in how to use these gifts to spread the gospel of Christ.

Through the Holy Spirit, God assigns spiritual gifts which when used together, form a unique body. Like a giant machine with hundreds of working gears and parts, the body of Christ becomes a "moving machine of the gospel". A machine taken apart cannot work properly nor will it get the proper results. Likewise, the body of Christ must be united in order to work together in the spreading of the love of God through His Son, Jesus Christ.

The family is a wonderful place to experience and share the love of Jesus. Within the family unit you will find not only love but competition, jealousy, desire for attention and pettiness. These are all part of normal family relations and when understood can strengthen and unify the family. Within the family unit of the church you will also find these same characteristics from which can come a realization of strength in unity. When strengths are recognized and unified, then the body is able to function and results will be seen.

As you study the lives of Martha and Mary you will observe the differences of gifts and how these two women were **Women of Worth** expressing their devotion in different ways. Both women loved the Lord and both showed their deep devotion to Him.

I. Martha the servant.

Martha expressed her love for Jesus and others by using her gift of hospitality. Her open home became a hub of spiritual activity. From her friendship with Jesus, Martha learned of eternal life and the value of being joyful in serving.

Read **Luke 10:38-41.** Write your comments about Martha, Mary, and Lazarus' home. _____

_____

_____

After Jesus began his public ministry at age 30 and until His death, it is not recorded that He returned to His natural home for rest and refreshment. Jesus loved the home of these three dear friends. His love is expressed with the most tender of emotions and He was obviously very comfortable being with this family. A Christian family is one of the most important representative examples of the love of God in our society.

As the home owner, Martha must have felt responsible for her guests and wanted to make sure that their needs were met. Relaxation, refreshment, renewal and rest were desperately needed by Jesus as He was moving into the heart of His ministry. Stress was beginning to be experienced by Him and the disciples.

How do you think Martha greeted her guests? How have you been greeted into different homes?_____

_____

Can you sense when there is coldness or tension in a home? _____

What do you think is meant by the term "distracted with much serving"?

_____

Was Martha's frustration with Mary justified? _____

_____

What about this family drew Jesus into such close friendship? How do you select your friends? _____

_____

_____

Proverbs 17:17a "A friend loves at all times."

II. Martha the student

Jesus was human. He had needs. He got tired, hungry, thirsty, and needful of relaxed interaction with friends. Just as Jesus was human, He was also divine. Daily He was unveiling His diety. Jesus took this opportunity to teach Martha a valuable lesson about priority. In doing this, He reveals a glimpse of Himself.

Read **Luke 10:41**. Comment on Jesus response to Martha's complaint. _____

_____

III. Martha the sorrowful

Jesus' broad ministry took him all over Judea and Galilee. At the time of Lazarus' sickness and death, He was approximately 25 miles away. Martha and Mary sent a messenger to Jesus to notify Him of the severity of Lazarus' illness.

Read **John 11:1-27.** Write your thoughts on how Martha must have felt.

_____

_____

Martha must have eagerly awaited the return of Jesus. She knew He would heal Lazarus as He had done with hundreds of others. Their home was filled with friends to offer support and help in caring for the dying Lazarus. Yet, her friends could not give what she needed. She knew that only Jesus could resolve this hopeless problem. Four days passed and Jesus didn't come! Then her brother died!

Death never comes as a welcome guest. Jesus uses this opportunity to reveal His deity and authority over life and death. God was to be glorified in a most incredible way.

Write your comments on Jesus' authority, timing and relationship with God.

_____

_____

_____

IV. Martha the satisfied.

Read **John 11:20-28.**

What does Martha's statement "I know that whatever you ask of God, God will give you" indicate about Martha's devotion to Jesus? _____

_____

Jesus reveals, especially to Martha a clear picture of His Lordship and asks the ultimate question of eternity.

John 11:25 "I am the resurrection and the life. He who believes in Me, though he may die, he shall live, and whoever lives and believes in Me shall never die. Do you believe this?"

What was Martha's response? _____

Read **John 11:28.** Comment on the phrase "and when she had said these things, she went on her way.....".

Jesus did not tell Martha that He was going to raise Lazarus from the dead. Martha was simply satisfied to know that Jesus' presence was all that was necessary to console her grieving heart. Not only did she receive comfort, but confidence to know that every need was going to be met by Jesus, both in this life and in the life to come. Jesus offered eternal hope.

Read **John 11:39-44**. Write your comments. _____

_____

_____

What can be learned from the life of Martha? Did she continue to use her gift as an honor unto the Lord? Read **John 12:2**. _____

_____

_____

_____

As the older sister, Martha was an example to Mary of service from devotion. She portrays an affluent woman who was respected in the community and appreciated because of her warmth and openness. After Martha met Jesus, she became more than a community servant, she became a servant of the Messiah. Jesus became her Lord and Master and because of this relationship, her service was enriched because she became an honor to God.

Martha opened her home to Jesus. Martha opened her heart to Jesus.

John 14:23 "If anyone loves Me, he will keep My Word; and My Father will love him, and We will come to him and make our home with him."

As you close this day, think on this, "How open to Jesus is my home and my heart?" Write a love prayer to Jesus.

Martha, Mary and Lazarus allow us into their home and their lives. We see three siblings who love Jesus and in their own unique ways express the depth of their love. They squabble and banter, but are a united force in the spread of the message of Jesus Christ.

Just as Martha expressed her love through her gift of hospitality, Mary expressed her love through the gift of evangelism which grew from her teachable spirit as she sat at the feet of Jesus. It is in that position that Mary gleaned and grew with every word that Jesus spoke.

Read **Luke 10:39**. Write your comments. _____

_____

I. Mary the teachable

Mary quickly learned that at the feet of Jesus was the best place to learn. Can you imagine the wisdom and knowledge that she must have heard from the lips of the Lord. How would you prepare if you knew that Jesus would be coming to your home for a visit? _____

_____

_____

What would you like to hear Jesus talk about if you could sit at His feet? _____

_____

_____

How do you think Mary responded to Martha's admonishment? _____

_____

Read **John 11:29-45**. Write your thoughts. _____

_____

_____

_____

Just as Mary gained from *sitting* at the feet of Jesus, in her deepest sorrow she found the greatest source of comfort by *falling* at His feet.

Read **John 11:35**. What does this verse mean to you?_____

_____

One of the most moving pictures of Jesus is with Martha and Mary as they are overcome by the sorrow of the death of Lazarus.

II. Mary the tender

Emotions are the window of the spirit.

> **Matthew 15:18a** "Those things which proceed out of the mouth come from the heart."

Comment on these emotions and how Mary expressed each one.

Happiness _____

Love _____

Frustration _____

Sorrow _____

Warmth _____

As Mary stood by Jesus can you imagine what must have gone through her mind as she heard the words "Lazarus, come forth!"? Her heart must have been beating so hard that her head was pounding with excitement.

III. Mary the testifier

Read **John 11:44-45**. Write your comments _____

_____

_____

_____

Mary must have been the more outgoing of the two sisters as we read where on several occasions the Jews followed Mary or came to her. She had a contagious personality and a persuasive ability in expressing her love for Jesus. Because of her testimony and the witness of her family, many believed in Him. She used her gift of evangelism.

IV. Mary the thankful

The final picture of Mary is again at the feet of Jesus. This time she is jubilantly and gratefully anointing Jesus' feet with oil.

1. She used very expensive oil representing the best she could offer.

2. She sat humbly at Jesus' feet symbolizing her yielded spirit.

3. She was unaware that she was preparing Jesus for His death.

4. The hate and deceit in the heart of Judas is revealed.

5. Mary's tender expression is the outpouring of a grateful heart.

As you prepare for your day of fast, pray and ask the Lord to make your heart tender and your love deep.

SEX is SPIRITUAL

To become a **Woman of Worth,** every area of your life must be open to what God says and there must be a willingness to be obedient to Him.

By way of review, consider God's **specific** will:

1. All individuals should come to know His Son, Jesus Christ. Week #3
2. A thankful attitude in all situations. (This is not impossible) Week #5

Another word from God about His **specific** will for your life is that you grow in Him and be pure in your concepts of sexuality. Read **I Thessalonians 4:3** and comment on this verse. _____

Along with the study of God's specific will, you studied areas that hinder a powerful prayer life. **Selfish motives** (Week #4) is one reason for unanswered prayer. **Sin** is another reason for a powerless prayer life. A third reason for unanswered prayer is impure **sexual attitudes.** The distorted view of love in our society has caused much confusion about sex. What is pure sex? What is impure sex?

Pornography, television sex, internet dating, sexually explicit magazines and homosexuality are examples of distorted viewpoints regarding love and sex. Love in our society has been cheapened and degraded because of the sexual lifestyles of the rich and famous. Politicians, athletes and religious leaders who live openly promiscuous lives continue to be role models in spite of their sexual indiscretions. Society has tried to redefine love and what is considered acceptable sexual behavior.

This casual approach to sex has also infiltrated the Christian community. According to George Barna, of the Barna Research Center, as many young women who attend church regularly are having sex outside marriage as those who do not attend church. Also, as many young women who attend church are having abortions as those who do not attend church. These statistics are heart breaking.

During this day of fasting and prayer, you will study love and sex in relationship to prayer. What does your attitude toward sex have to do with prayer? **A healthy view of sex is vitally important to your relationship with God.**

105

Love is the ultimate Bible word.

> **I John 4:8** "He who does not love does not know God, for God is love."

God shows His love for you on a daily basis. He wants you to experience life and love at its fullest as an extension of His love. There are three types of love expressed throughout the Bible.

Agape - the love of God for man and man's ability to return love to God
Philos - the love expressed through friendship
Eros - the love between a man and woman

Read **I Corinthians 13**. Can you identify 15 aspects of true love?

Your attitude regarding love is the foundation on which all relationships are established. How do you express love to God? How do you express love to a friend? How should you express intimate love?

Sex is the expression of intimate love between a man and woman. When sex is experienced outside of marriage, God does not approve and therefore it will hinder your relationship with Him. God established the relationship between male and female from the beginning to be innocent, pure, intimate and passionate. Not only does it replenish the earth, but unites a man and woman in a relationship the Bible calls "**one**". The principle is "**one man for one woman**". This is God's only approved expression of sex. Write your thoughts on this principle.

Read **Matthew 19:4-6**. Write your comments. _____

_____

_____

Sex outside marriage is disobedience and therefore sin.

In the book of the Song of Solomon, Solomon gives a detailed account of the love and union he had with the Shulamite maiden. In this beautiful love story he describes a picture of the beauty of the sexual experience.

Three resources have been given by God to help you understand and clarify sensitive subjects such as sex.

1. God's Word clearly defines sexual attitudes and behavior.
2. Prayer is God's way to communicate His thoughts to you.
3. The Holy Spirit will help you to stay pure in your sexual behavior.

Read again **I Thessalonians 4:1-4**. Write your comments._____

_____

What does the term "sexual purity" mean to you? Is virginity important? Why or why not? _____

_____

_____

God put into each of us the desire to be loved and to experience sex. You have a need to give and receive love passionately and intimately. God explained in His Word the proper way to express these wonderful emotions.

Read **Genesis 1:27-28; 31**. Write your comments. _____

_____

The Word says that God "blessed them" meaning that He saw what He had created and from this blessing created the ability to procreate (make babies). Sex is meant to be a blessing to God and to a man and woman. Also as God viewed the man and woman and their union, He saw "it was **VERY** good."

SEX is a SPIRITUAL experience.

In the right context, love between a man and woman is a union beyond your wildest imagination. **It is blessed by God!** God wants the sexual relationship to be the highest expression of the intimacy of deep love and passion.

Marriage is the right context for sex.

The temptation to have sex outside marriage is overwhelming. The availability of birth control and abortion makes it easy to avoid unwanted pregnancy. The portrayal of sex by movies and television makes perverted sex seem normal and acceptable. The false notion that "everyone does it" is part of the ideology of the humanistic view of sexuality. Sex is pictured as an acceptable way to express appreciation for a "good date". The biblical explanation of sex is that it comes as the apex of love and the unifying of a man and woman in marriage.

Some of the concepts of biblical sex:

1. Sex is good! - **Genesis 5:1-2**
2. Sex is fulfilling! - **Genesis 29:20**
3. Sex is productive! - **I Samuel 1:19-20**
4. Sex is satisfying! - **Song of Solomon 2:16**
5. Sex is relaxing! - **Song of Solomon 4:6**
6. Sex is intimate! - **Song of Solomon 7:10**
7. Sex is a seal! - **Song of Solomon 8:6-7**
8. Sex is unifying! - **Matthew 19:6**
9. Sex is a blessing! - **Genesis 1:28**

Sex is the most intimate part of a woman and the most intimate part of a man coming together. When you come together in the biblical sense, you are joined physically, emotionally, relationally and most of all spiritually.

As a teenager can you be strong and withstand the temptation and pressure to be sexually active? You must set your standards regarding sex early!

It is easy to say, "NO!" to a nerd, but hard to handle a hunk!

As a young woman, can you be patient and trust God to bring you the man that is especially designed to be your partner?

Don't rush God! His timing is perfect!

As a married woman, can you stay committed and under the blessings of God, relax and enjoy the romance and beauty of the sexual act?

Sex in marriage is a blessing to God!

As you fast today, pray that the Lord will clarify your ideas regarding love and sexual purity and show you the beauty of the spiritual sexual experience in contrast to the self seeking, world view of sex.

You may need to consider these questions.

Have I been sexually impure in thought or action?
Do I watch sexually suggestive programs which arouse my sexual desires?
Am I dating someone who is pressuring me to be active sexually?
Have I committed adultery?
Have I had an abortion?
Is my relationship centered around sex and physical satisfaction?
Am I making excuses for my sexual behavior?
Since I don't enjoy being intimate, am I withholding from my husband something that God has blessed? Am I selfish in the area of sex?

You need to know this:

God made you with sexual desires and passions.
God wants you to be fulfilled sexually.
God can change your concepts regarding sex.
God can break the bondage of sexual impurity.
God will restore you, if you confess and commit to purity.

If you have been or are involved in impure sexual behavior, you must confess this as sin and ask God to forgive you and then make a commitment to study and learn about biblical love and proper sexual behavior. Just as God created man and woman He created love and sex.

Read **James 4:17** and **I John 1:9**. Write your comments. _____

_____

Close this day of fasting and prayer with a prayer of thanksgiving for the intimacy that God has given and of His great love for you. Pray that your expressions of love will be pleasing to God in every way.

Observations Regarding Devotion

God intended for the home to be a place of love, warmth, acceptance, rest, encouragement and support. It was established from the beginning that the family and home be the perfect place to express the deep emotions of the spirit. The home is to be a retreat center from the pressures of life. Each family member brings a unique personality to the family structure. God's plan is for each family member to grow and develop their special individual abilities and gifts and then come together in the perfect expression of devotion.

God's devotion to us and our devotion to our family is an eternal concept.

God is totally devoted to helping your family grow and develop. To be blessed by God, the family must be devoted to each other and unite together to serve like Martha and sit at His feet like Mary.

The home of Martha, Mary and Lazarus was a special home. However, it was a normal home, filled with activity, rivalry and disagreements. The fact that Jesus was part of their home shows that He can bring an element of peace as He becomes the intermediary between the individual members of the family.

Jesus' presence in a home will unify the family!

When the personalities of the family clash, it provides the opportunity to express love, forgiveness, reconciliation and restoration. These are examples, of the extension of the personality of God; loving, forgiving and reconciling.

How should these emotions be expressed within the family? Write your thoughts.

Love   Reconciliation
Mercy   Restoration
Forgiveness   Friendship
Acceptance   Encouragement
Discipline   Support

Martha, Mary and Lazarus' home was an open place where friendship was shared, food was enjoyed and the gospel was presented.

As the elder sibling, what strengths and weaknesses does Martha reveal?

_____

_____

Martha's devotion to Jesus is clear. Her way of expressing love to Jesus was by **action** and **service**. Mary's devotion to Jesus was just as deep. Yet her way of expressing love to Jesus was in **receiving** and **sharing.** It was normal for Martha to be a bit envious of Mary who found sitting more inspirational than serving. Both Martha and Mary's expressions of devotion are examples of different ways to use your abilities.

Without Martha's warm openness, her home could not have developed into a hub of activity where people felt free to come meet Jesus and spend time in fellowship with Him. As she cleaned her home and prepared for the meals, she was expressing her love for Jesus by using her unique ability of hospitality.

Without Mary's winsome personality, many of the Jews may not have come to know Christ. Her magnetic personality indicates that she was able to interest people in Jesus and willing to invite people to come to her house to meet Him.

Martha trusted Jesus. Her devotion to Jesus is shown through her acts of service. As her hands quickly prepared food for an unexpected entourage of travelers, we can assume that she was well organized and prepared to meet any need of the hungry, tired and searching who might enter her home. She seemed to be content even when there were many guests, and they arrived unexpectedly.

As the younger sister, what strengths and weaknesses do you see in Mary?

_____

_____

How did these sisters unite to become a moving force for the spreading of the gospel?

_____

Mary was tender and open and her heart of devotion was expressed through her sharing the love of Jesus with others. She most assuredly shared openly of her love for Christ, of how He had changed her life and the life of her family. She probably exploded with excitement as she shared how peace had come to her life and how joy had consumed her heart. The fragrant perfume which she used to anoint Jesus' feet must have filtered through the room. This exercise of love was a public display of the testimony of her deep devotion to the Lord Jesus.

Every individual gift is necessary to the kingdom purpose of God.

The reputation of the family has a great impact on the community. The home of Martha, Mary and Lazarus depicts a respected family with great influence. As the family unites, it becomes stronger and more influential.

Read **John 12: 9-11**. Write your comments. _____

_____

_____

_____

_____

Because of the raising of Lazarus from the dead, many people were curious about Jesus and who He was. Many lives were changed for eternity as some came to salvation because of Martha, Mary and Lazarus' family influence. However, it also brought opposition. Questions began to arise and problems soon occurred endangering all the followers of Jesus. Yet Martha, Mary and Lazarus remain steadfast in their devotion.

A family that unites to take a stand for Christ can expect negative comments and open criticism.

As you close this day, pray for your family to become a public influence for Christ by your love and devotion to each other and to Jesus Christ.

Personal Applications - Devotion

Review the special abilities of Martha and Mary and list your special personality traits and abilities. _____

_____

_____

_____

_____

Your home may or may not be an influence for Jesus Christ, but as a family member, you can become more devoted to strengthening your family and encouraging the other members as they relate within the family.

What are the strengths and weaknesses of each member of your family?

Make a list by name of each of your family members and how you will commit to pray for them to become stronger in the Lord.

Do you use your home as an open witness for Christ? _____

_____

How can you become an encourager to the members of your family? _____

_____

_____

Everyone is devoted to someone or something.

If there are frequent clashes in your home, perhaps you can become more sensitive to problem areas and try to avoid confrontation. You may be the only believer in your family and there may be open hostility to your faith in Christ. If this is the case, you can be strengthened through prayer and commitment to God's word daily. If you are unmarried, when you establish a home and family, you can begin your family on a solid foundation.

There is great pressure on the homes of our society. A battle for the defeat

> **Psalm 127:1** "Unless the Lord builds the house, they labor in vain who build it."

of the family is being fought between the evil forces of Satan and the angels of God. Satan wants families to fail and then carry the guilt and baggage of the failed family relationship for the rest of their lives. It often seems easier to "walk out rather than work it out" when problems exist. It takes courage, strength and devotion from a **Woman of Worth** to stay and fight for her family. A weakened family unit can only be strong with the power of God. When a family falls apart there is hurt and blame. Bitterness and anger are sometimes carried from the broken home into the establishing of a new home. Divorce has become commonplace and the blended family has become a common phrase.

Read **Nehemiah 4:14**. Write your comments. _____

_____

_____

_____

You are a warrior fighting for your family.
As the home goes, so goes the nation.
You can overcome a failed family relationship through the power of God.
The home is intended to be filled with love, understanding and forgiveness.
As God has given you mercy, you can likewise be merciful to your family.

A family can only be blended when it is united with the love of Christ.

Your home is not an experiment station for society.

The new phrase "starter marriages" is a catchy term for trial marriage. God did not intend the home to become an experiment station for society. He wants the home to be a place of wonder and excitement, love and commitment. Two people who come together under the Lordship of Christ, both individually seeking to have a personal intimate relationship with Him and then uniting to form a home, have begun under the blessings of God.

Read **Matthew 19:3-9**. Write your comments _____

_____

_____

_____

When God's design for a home is followed, it is more likely that the home can survive the trials and stresses of family life. Anytime your family faces a challenge it becomes an opportunity to seek the power and strength of the Lord. As your family seeks the Lord and faces the situation together, you become a testimony to your friends and neighbors of how God works in your home.

Just as the home of Martha, Mary and Lazarus became a lighthouse of hope and a beacon to the community, so your home can be a place of rest, refreshment and relaxation. As you become confident in Christ as a **Woman of Worth,** you will be able to see more clearly how you can fit into God's kingdom plan to reach a world for Christ using your life and home.

A prayer to end your week: Oh Lord, thank You for giving me my family. Help me to use the abilities and gifts that You have blessed me with to reach people with Your love. Please bless my home and remind me that only when a home is set on the foundation of Your love and mercy can it be a blessing to others. Let my family see Your love through my life. I love you, Lord.

Thank you!

Your Thoughts:

Becoming
a
Woman of Worth

WEEK # 7

LEADER

BECOMING A WOMAN OF WORTH

LEADER

Week # 7 - **Deborah** - Lesson #1

Principle: A strong leader must be courageous and bold!

To become a **Woman of Worth** you must learn to face life with courage. Each of the women studied both from the Old Testament and New Testament are representative of all women. Women who faced challenges, problems, hurts, sorrows and joys. Sometimes these women felt "on top of the world", completely confident in their situations. At other times we sense their feelings of insecurity and unimportance.

Your strengths can become your vulnerabilities. Learning to handle relationships is critical. It is hard to get over being hurt. Friendships are fragile. Strong women are sometimes a threat to society. How can you truly be a strong, stable, secure, confident Christian woman and still be submissive and supportive?

You may ask "How do I stay calm when crisis comes? There are so many problems in my life. My job takes so much energy and time. It is placing pressure on my family. I have strong leadership qualities, but I don't have anyone who is supportive of my strengths. What should I do? Should I just give in and not exert my strong characteristics even though I know God gave me these qualities to become all that He wants me to be? He made me the way I am, right?"

As you look at the life of Deborah, you will study her leadership skills and the importance of developing and using the qualities of strength, courage and intelligence in becoming a **Woman of Worth.**

119

There have been many women in history who became leaders and illustrate the courage and savvy needed to make a difference in society. Some of these women experienced opposition from their peers and had to go against the norm of their generation, to move forward and forge paths for women of the future.

Women have been monumental in the changing of laws regarding voter rights, and in seeking equal pay for equal work in the job market. Women have been successful in advancements in medicine, athletics, space exploration and in the pursuit of peace. Women such as Joan of Arc, Clara Barton, Susan B. Anthony, and Sally Ride are known for their contributions to womenhood.

But what about the women of Christian history who set the example of devotion, commitment and inspiration? From the "in the beginning" in **Genesis 1:1** to the "surely I come quickly" in **Revelation 22:20,** there have been women who have been bold and courageous.

It takes a special woman to rise above the norm and be a leader.

Read **Psalm 31:24**. Write your thoughts about the courage and boldness of these women:

Sarah - **Genesis 21:1-7**
Jochebed - **Exodus 2:1-10**
Ruth - **Ruth 1:16-18**
Abigail - **I Samuel 25:23; 32-35**
Lydia - **Acts 16:13-15**
Priscilla - **Acts 18:2; 26**

How have you become the woman you are today? _____

_____

Who has influenced your life to this point? _____

Who would you list as role models for your life? Why?_____

_____

120

The book of Judges is a time of dark history in the Bible. The pattern of rebellion, retribution, repentance, restoration and rest continues for 350 years. During this time there are 13 individuals who attempt to lead Israel but with limited success. Deborah was the only woman judge that God raised up to give advice and leadership to this depraved and needy people.

I. Deborah the prophetess.

We know little about Deborah's family heritage. There are only a few women God granted the privilege to be called "prophetess". Through the prophets God communicated His direction and truths to the people. As Deborah's reputation as an advisor grew, great numbers of people would come to her for advise and counsel. One question they may have asked is "Is God angry with us?" or "Why has God forgotten us?"

Read **Judges 2:10-16**. How quickly can God be forgotten? _____

Why was the Lord angry? _____

_____

Read **Judges 3:4**. Why did the Lord leave enemies for Israel to face?

_____

Do you think it was difficult for Deborah to speak God's truth? _____

_____

What do you think she may have said? _____

_____

What type of personality must Deborah have had in order to have commanded such respect and admiration? _____

_____

The name "Deborah" means "bee". Just as a bee symbolizes hard work, active behavior, and organization, it also symbolizes a "sting". The bee is capable of both "sweet honey" and a "stinging hurt". How does she illustrate these qualities?

_____

Research your name and if possible find out how you were given this name. Find out about the meaning of your name. _____

_____

II. Deborah the married woman.

Some have said that her husband, Lapidoth must have been a wimp, weak "hen pecked" man. However, his name, even though in the original Hebrew is used in the feminine gender, means "torches" or "lightning flashes" signifying a quiet, yet strong, supportive man. Do you know men who are quiet yet have an inner strength that supersedes their quietness?

What problems could the fact that she was married have presented? _____

_____

How important was the personality of Lapidoth? How do you think God used him in Deborah's life? _____

_____

How could children have made a difference to Lapidoth and Deborah? _____

_____

How important to a relationship is mutual respect and support? How did this help affirm Deborah in her strong leadership role? _____

It has been said that behind every great man there is a great woman. In this case, behind this great powerful warrior leader there is an exceptionally strong supportive man!

III. **Deborah the introspective**

In order for Deborah to give sound advice, she had to know God in an intimate way. She praised and acknowledged the power of God over the enemy. She blessed God for giving direction and victory in battle.

Read **Judges 5:1-2.** Comment on Deborah's relationship with God.

How important is a personal relationship to God in being a strong leader?

_____

IV. **Deborah the bold**

Read **Judges 4:6.** Comment on the statement she made to Barak as she called him to lead the Israelites to battle. _____

_____

What were the odds against the Hebrews? _____

Did the fact that they would be outnumbered seem to bother or frighten Deborah?

_____

> **I Chronicles 20:15b; 17** " Do not be afraid nor dismayed because of this great multitude, for the battle is not yours, but God's."

Read **Judges 4:6-7.** Write your thoughts on what God said about the outcome of the battle.

_____

_____

It takes courage to declare victory before the battle is fought!

Jabin of Canaan, enemy of Israel had oppressed them for 20 years. His commander, Sisera was in charge of an army of 900 chariots and as many as 100,000 warriors. Even though they were far outnumbered, the victory had already been given to Deborah and Barak. God said so! That made it so!

V. **Deborah the tactful**

Read **Judges 4:8-9.** Write your thoughts on Barak's reaction to Deborah's call to battle and on Deborah's response to Barak. _____

_____

What do you think of the statement in **Judges 4:9b** "for the Lord will sell Sisera into the hand of a woman"? _____

_____

VI. **Deborah the brave**

Deborah reveals a brave-hearted warrior, not eager for combat, but ready to "stay the course" and battle the enemy alongside her people.

Read **Judges 4:15-24**. Write your thoughts. _____

_____

_____

_____

Deborah illustrates a wise leader who was courageous and bold. Jael illustrates a strong woman who acts out of loyalty and faithfulness to her people. She was cunning, deceitful and murderous. Could she have handled the situation with Sisera any differently? _____

_____

Desperate situations often lead to hasty reactions.

VI. **Deborah the poet**

The Song of Deborah is a fine example of Hebrew poetry. Deborah recaps again through poetry and praise the battle with Jabin and Sisera and how God gave them victory.

Read **Judges 5:1-31**. Write Deborah's words of praise.

How did God use nature to help in the battle? _____

_____

Read **Judges 5:10-11**. Write your thoughts about the victory.

_____

_____

Take this time to write a poem of praise.

_____

_____

_____

_____

_____

_____

_____

   As you close this day to prepare for your day of fasting, ask the Lord if your approach to life is pleasing to Him. Are you attempting to do the right thing, but with limited success because you are trying to do what pleases you rather than what pleases God? Do you act out of haste before you consider asking the Lord for help? Thank Him for His mercy and that with Him you can be courageous and bold. Read your poem aloud as a prayer.

LIVING DOUBT FREE

As you fast and pray today, you will study the importance of being a life-witness. It is important to know that someones' ideas about God may be the result of the life-witness that you have given them. It is true that "You may be the only Bible that someone reads". Their whole concept of God; His love, forgiveness, grace and mercy may be defined by what they see in your life.

Just as God has said it is His will that you be saved through Jesus Christ, have a thankful heart and be pure, He has also said that He wants you to have a life-witness that brings glory to Him and reflects positively on His Holiness.

I Peter 2:15 " For this is the will of God, that by doing good you may put to silence the ignorance of foolish men."

How is your life reflecting the will of God? Do you have a sweet spirit?
Are you kind to others? Are you being a good friend?
Are you eager to volunteer to help out someone in need?
Do you show mercy and forgiveness when you have been hurt?
Are you displaying the fruit of the spirit?

> **I Peter 1:15-16** "but as He who called you is holy, you also be holy in all your conduct, because it is written, 'Be holy, for I am holy'".

Read **Galatians 5:22-23** - List the fruit of the spirit.

As you reflect on your life-witness, also reflect on your prayer life. Have you identified areas where there is a lack of power? Did you identify some selfish motives or sinful behaviors? It may be that none of these are a problem in your prayer life. Maybe it is a lack of faith. Do you doubt God?

One of the primary reasons for a powerless prayer life is lack of faith and **doubt.**

Read and compare **Hebrews 11:6** and **James 1:6-8**_____

Deborah is an example of a bold courageous woman who knew the strength she had been given was directly from God. She praised God and then trusted in His direction in doing battle with the enemy. The odds were poor, her army was not as well equipped, her leader had to be encouraged by her presence, the morale was low, but she did not doubt God because her faith was strong.

What makes a person have doubt? Does God not make Himself clear through His Word? Why is doubt so common?

Satan is the originator of doubt. He knows that once you are secure in Christ (saved), your eternal destiny is settled. However, if Satan can plant the seeds of doubt in your mind, then you are immediately rendered ineffective as a life-witness for Jesus. It is a fact! You won't share your trust and faith in Christ when you have doubt.

Read **Matthew 28:17-18**. Comment on what you think the disciples were doubting? _____

_____

Some questions often asked:

"How can the Bible be true when there are so many other writings?"
"How can horrible things happen in the world if God is loving?"
"How can Jesus be the only way to relate to God?"
"How could Jesus give His life for such a person as me?"
"Who am I to think that I am worth anything to anyone?"

Some people frequently doubt their salvation. Some factors which cause doubt are fear, indecision, sin, impatience, rationalization and logic.

Read **Matthew 18:3-4**. Write your thoughts. _____

_____

If you have ever had a personal encounter with Jesus, you have no need to doubt.

127

I am sure you have observed a trusting toddler jump from a high place into the safety of the arms of an adoring father. The child will not doubt that he will be caught. He will not rationalize. He won't stop to think nor ask, "Are you going to catch me? How can I be sure? It is so high. You don't look very strong to me. If I fall, I might get hurt and have to go to the hospital." A child raised in a loving adoring environment will not doubt.

1. A secure child will not hesitate to trust a parent.
2. A trusting child believes what he/she is told.
3. A loved child is secure and does not doubt authority.
4. An obedient child will obey their parent.

> **Matthew 18:3** "Assuredly, I say to you, unless you are converted and become as little children, you will by no means enter the kingdom of Heaven. Therefore whoever humbles himself as this little child is the greatest in the kingdom of heaven."

As your loving father, God wants you to trust Him with this same type of assurance. No need to question! God has revealed through His word that anyone can have confidence in His love.

Read these scriptures and write why you should not doubt.

John 5:24
John 10:27-30
Romans 8:15-17
Ephesians 1:13-14
I John 5:10-13

When you doubt, you are saying more about yourself than you are saying about God.
There are many uncertain things in life, but these things are sure:

1. God is always faithful.
2. His Word is always true and reveals His faithfulness.
3. You can count on Him.
4. You have no need to doubt.

As you end this day of fasting and prayer, write a prayer of thanksgiving that God has given you His word to assure you of His presence in your life.

Observations Regarding Leadership

There has been much controversy over women in leadership roles. We live in an era in history where women have more rights and are treated more equally than ever before. Businesses are successfully owned by women. Women are involved in politics, athletics, media, medicine, finance and technology. Women serve in the armed forces alongside men. Women command ships and pilot planes. Is it possible for a woman to be a successful career woman and be equally successful at home as a wife and mother? It takes a woman of courage and boldness to meet the challenge of leadership; a woman who knows who she is and where she is headed, in other words a **Woman of Worth.**

One area of heated debate is concerning women in leadership in the church. Should women pastor churches? Should women be in authority over men? Where do women fit into the Kingdom Plan of God?

Whenever questions are raised that bring confusion into your Christian life, you must study, pray and seek the face of God until clarity comes. Part of the responsibility of the Holy Spirit is to lead you into truth and to guide you with wisdom. As you consider the life of Deborah, consider how she was used by God.

What do you think might have happened if Deborah had not courageously and boldly taken the leadership position? Consider:

Deborah was the leader of the Hebrew nation.
Deborah was the prominent person in her marriage.
Deborah was gifted by God as a prophetess.
Deborah was sought for wisdom and guidance.
God used Deborah to unify the people and bring victory in battle.
Because of her leadership, there was rest in the land for 40 years.
Deborah stated God's command clearly to Barak.
Deborah attempted to lead Barak to come to his potential as a leader.
Deborah attempted to step into a supportive role and allow Barak to lead.
Barak was told what the outcome would be if he did not lead.

What would have happened if Barak had accepted and taken the role of primary leader? Would Deborah have stayed behind to wait the return of the victorious army? Consider:

Barak had the qualifications to be the leader of the army of God.
Barak knew what God had said.
Deborah wanted Barak to take the primary role in battle.
Barak was satisfied to be the second in command.
Barak stated his dependence on Deborah.

Deborah and Barak came together minimizing their inabilities and maximizing their abilities. The example that Deborah and Barak gave is one of the combining of male and female leadership cooperating to fulfill the plan of God. These are two very gifted and strong individuals who have the capabilities of leading alone, yet by coming together their strengths are used to the fullest and God is glorified through the victory of the battle.

Deborah proves her greatest leadership skill when she states, "Bless the Lord! I will sing praise to the Lord God of Israel." In seeking the Lord, knowing what He says, and being willing to be obedient, she provides a superb example of leadership for all women to follow.

Five leadership principles

1. Acknowledge God as sovereign.
2. Establish a personal relationship with God based on thanksgiving.
3. Be available to be used of God.
4. Pursue a knowledge of God's word.
5. Obey and follow God's direction.

Five leadership characteristics

1. Wisdom
2. Trustworthy
3. Courageous
4. Bold
5. Humble

Personal Applications - Leadership

What type of leader are you? What kind of personality do you have? Are you an assertive, straight forward, take charge woman? Or are you a quiet, shy, in the background woman? There is a need for both types of leadership skills. What does God want to accomplish through your life?

The truly successful leader has the ability to bring out the best in those around them. Do you bring out the best in those around you? Can you lead with strength, yet remain humble and kind? Can you make wise decisions which take courage and boldness, yet maintain your grace and dignity as a woman?

Which takes more leadership skills, the leader who leads with aggression, pride and forcefulness or the leader who leads with strength undergirded by grace and dignity?

It takes courage and boldness to know when to lead and when to back away. You need to know how to work together with others to present a strong force. Someone has to be the leader whether in war, business, church or family. Herein lies the battle between the sexes; **who's going to be in control?**

In your personal relationships, consider the design of God!

I. Leadership in the home.

God's original intent was for the man to be the leader and the woman to come along side as his "helper companion". Man was created to lead in the spiritual development, emotional health and financial security of the relationship and she created to add strength, support and softness to unify and balance. As the man and woman seek God as individuals, then they can join their unique personalities and outstanding abilities to become the foundation of society.

Read **Genesis 2:18**. Write your comments. _____

_____

Read **Genesis 3:16-24**. Write your thoughts. _____

_____

_____

What went wrong? Where is the conflict between man and woman?

Eve should have passed the question along to Adam and asked for his input. She didn't think about the result of taking one small bite and how this choice would alter the direction of their lives. The outcome of one wrong decision is still haunting society. What would have happened if Eve had not yielded to the temptation to eat of the fruit of the tree of the knowledge of good and evil?

What would have happened if Adam had not followed after Eve? We see that his decision to join Eve set in motion the **"control factor"** for all ages. She fell to temptation and by doing so, took control of the decision . He relinquished the responsibility that God had given him to be the leader when he complied with Eve.

We live in a fallen world. Perhaps we would have responded the same as Adam and Eve. Even when we do become confused about the design for man and woman, God's word gives guidance and instruction on how to correct these decisions and live harmoniously under God's blessings and mercy.

In your profession, examine your motives!

II. Leadership in the job.

Was God's design that man should work and woman stay at home?

Read **Proverbs 31:16-31**. Write your thoughts. _____

_____

Read **Acts 16:14**. Write your thoughts. _____

_____

Both these women were smart, industrious and business minded. Many families in our society are two income families. If it weren't for these combined efforts, the family would suffer financially. Some women have high profile jobs, some run their own businesses, some make enormous salaries and are in control of numbers of employees.

The attitude you have toward work is imperative to the responses and reactions that you will get from the people around you.

Have you selected this career because of personal desire, ego and pride or is it because you want to use your abilities to please God? Do you seek to gain advancement professionally to fulfill some void in your life? Do you consider your vocation as a way of bringing strength to relationships? How will you react if at some point your job begins to conflict with your relationships in the home? You will need to consider the time and energy that your vocation will require. Will you have anything left to give to the responsibilities of home and family? Can you be efficient in every area without neglecting something?

In seeking God's choice for your vocation, you must be clear in not only knowing your abilities but in knowing where God will utilize your skills and what type of job He wants you to have.

In the church, think about what is best for the church body.

III. Leadership in the church.

Another area of intense conflict is in leadership in the church. Should there be women pastors? Where do women fit into God's Kingdom Plan? Should women be in authority over men?

Women were a vital part of the ministry of Jesus. Jesus raised the status of women. Write your thoughts on these verses.

Mark 16:9 - The risen Lord appeared first to Mary Magdalene.
Luke 8:1-3 - Women were involved in Jesus' ministry.
John 4:9 - He spoke to the Samaritan woman.
John 11:5 - He was best friends with women.
Acts 1:12-14 - Women were involved in preparation for Pentecost.

Through the three years of Jesus' ministry, He gave us the revelation of Himself as Messiah, the gift of eternal salvation, the design of discipleship and the plan for the future of His church. He gave no example, told no parable, or made no direct statement to indicate the place of women in ministry. However, He did leave strong impressions.

Mary Magdalene was the first to tell of Jesus' resurrection.
Mary, the sister of Martha, introduced others to Jesus.
Jesus did not have a woman as one of the twelve disciples.
At Pentecost, women were involved in the prayer ministry.
In the New Testament church, women opened the way for evangelism.

Women were important in every aspect of the ministry of Jesus. They ministered through evangelism, financial support, hospitality and friendship. He lifted women in ministry to a place of significance, but did not place women in the primary position of leading the body.

Can women adequately perform all aspects of ministry? Yes, women are just as capable in all avenues of ministry. **Ability is not the issue, control is.**

Perhaps the difficulty lies in the desire of women to be in control. We need to examine our motives in doing what we do in leadership.

The main goal of all church leaders should **always** be to glorify God in order to attract people to a life in Christ and then to disciple them so that they will grow in their personal relationship with God through His son, Jesus Christ.

Many children would not be active in church nor come to Christ if women had not been diligent in teaching and leading in the church. Often it is the mother who takes the role of spiritual leader in the home because the father does not.

To repeat, the truly successful leader desires to bring out the best in those around them. **God's design is for men to lead and women to support.** Both are vital to the growth and development of the Kingdom of God.

Examine your views of women in leadership by thoroughly studying the examples given throughout scripture.

The woman who had the greatest opportunity to step into a primary position in the birth and development of the New Testament church was Mary the mother of Jesus. She was not only the mother of our Lord, she was with Him daily and was responsible for His care and guidance. How do you think it might have been to be Jesus' mother?

Read **Acts 1:1-14**. Write your thoughts. _____

_____

_____

At the gathering of the "body, the believers in Christ" just after Jesus went back into heaven and just before Pentecost, we see a beautiful picture of the development of the church and the leadership.

What assignment did Jesus give to the believers?
What strength is seen in the body as they gathered together?
Who came forward as the spokesperson for the group?
What place did the women assume in this meeting?

As you close this week of study regarding courage and boldness in leading, be prayerful about what God wants for your life. Ask yourself these questions.

How can I best glorify God with my life?
What is God's best design for marriage, family and work?
Who would I want to be the spiritual head of my relationships?
Do the words submission and leadership contrast or combine?
What is in the best interest of those under my influence?

A prayer to end your week: Oh Lord, teach me Your ways. Guide me in understanding Your design for my life. Help me to use my strengths to bring glory and honor to You. Let me know where I am weak and help me to place my weaknesses under Your control. Help me to encourage those in my life to become all that You want them to be. Help me to lead with a humble spirit always remembering from where my strength comes.

                                        You are Lord of all!

Your Thoughts:

Becoming
a
Woman of Worth

WEEK # 8

CONSECRATED

BECOMING A WOMAN OF WORTH

CONSECRATED

Week # 8 - **Dorcas (Tabitha) and Phoebe** - Lesson #1

Principle: Holiness is a life-long pursuit!

As you become a **Woman of Worth** you will learn new things about yourself based on what you are learning about God. He wants you to know Him intimately. His holiness. His grace. His mercy. His forgiveness. His tenderness. His love. His goodness. His strength. His power. All these parts of His personality and so much more are available to you. Your life can be richer, fuller and more meaningful with each new experience. As you know more about the life and work of Jesus and the Holy Spirit, you will become more intune with God and His plan for your life.

The word consecration is defined as "to set apart as holy; dedicated". Part of the confidence you gain in Christ is to know that every new day is a new adventure with God. He empowers your life; He reveals your worth. He develops your character and He overshadows your problems by guiding you through each new challenge. By knowing Him, you come to know more of His great love and of His desire for you to become all that you can be.

Part of worth is realizing that you are not holy, but He is!

Your personal worth can not be measured in tangible ways. You are more valuable than money. You are more precious than jewels. You are more lovely than the blossoms of spring. You are more beautiful than the colors of the rainbow.

You are special!

You are so valuable to God that no one can be you. No one can fulfill the special task that God has for you, like you can. God will see that the plan for His Kingdom is completed and He will use available individuals to carry this out. However, He has a special task for you in His Kingdom Plan that is designed especially with you and your special uniqueness in mind. The choices that you make; marriage or not, children or not, what type of job, where you attend church, your friendships, the neighborhood in which you live, your moral and social decisions all can be used by God to enrich your life and the lives of others under your influence. Your talents, abilities and personality are gifts designed by God specifically for you to bless Him and others.

The question remains, "What are you doing with your life? Do you **Know** that you are worth more than you can ever imagine to the King of Kings and Lord of Lords.

How wonderful you must be that He loves you so!

You will never be able to gain enough approval from those around you to satisfy your needs. All the advancements of your vocation; more money, a better promotion, more responsiblity, more perks can not give you selfworth. The love of your family and your friends can not make you feel worthwhile. Your community service and the respect of your peer group will not satisfy the deep desire of your soul. Recreation, social interaction, even church activity can not make you content. You will continue to have deep yearnings within the innerpart of your soul until you plug into the only source of satisfaction.

The void of self worth will remain empty until filled with the presence and power of the Holiness of God.

Read **Luke 11:9-10**. Write your thoughts. _____

_____

All that is necessary to become the **Woman of Worth** that God intends you to be is your dedication. Ask, seek, and knock and He will open the windows of heaven and pour out on you blessings that you can never count.

As we complete this study in **Becoming a Woman of Worth,** you will look at the lives of two women. Both of these women were unique and special and they reflect how God used their talent, ability and especially their availabilty to spread His message of love. **These women were contagious Christians.** They lived their lives in Christ.

When the church exploded after Pentecost, thousands of people came to Christ. Cell churches were springing up meeting under trees, by rivers, in homes, and in businesses. People were drawn to the changed lives. They were eager to know Jesus. **The greatest witness for Christ is a changed life.**

Read **Acts 9:36-43**. Write your thoughts._____

_____

_____

I. Dorcas - A disciple

What is the definition of "a disciple"? _____

_____

How can you identify "a disciple"? _____

Read **Matthew 7:20**. Write your thoughts. _____

_____

II. Dorcas - A good person

When you think of a good person, who comes to mind?_____

_____

What do you think Luke meant when he said "full of good works"?_____

_____

Dorcas was filled with inner fruit which was expressed through her good works.

Inner fruit bears outer fruit!

III. Dorcas - A charitable nature

How was Dorcas' ability used as a witness for Christ? _____

_____

Many women were influenced by the sewing talents of Dorcas. As they discussed the pattern and fabric and took the measurements, she must have shared about her new relationship with Jesus Christ. When the ladies returned for a fitting, she certainly would have shared about what Christ was doing in her life and as she delivered the finished garment, she would not forget to thank her clients and mention how her life was being blessed daily by Jesus.

Her death must have filled her friends, neighbors and clients with grief. Have you experienced the death of family member or close friend? What emotions did you have? _____

The special visit by Peter and the miracle of Dorcas being raised from the dead sent shock waves throughout Joppa. Can you imagine the opportunities that this event provided for witnessing? Whenever there are unexplainable miracles, it provides the perfect opportunity to turn the topic back to a testimony about Jesus.

What do you think Dorcas said after being resurrected?_____

_____

How can experiences like this be turned into witnessing opportunities? _____

_____

_____

Dorcas' sewing needle was the tool that she used to open the door for witnessing about Jesus. What "tools" can you use?

142

Week # 8 - Lesson # 2

Read **Romans 16:1-2**. Write your thoughts. _____

_____

_____

I. Phoebe - Sister

Throughout Paul's missionary journeys, he learned of the necessity of the lay people being involved in continuing the ministries that he had begun. Besides disciplining the new converts, sometimes he would ask one of his lay leaders to deliver a letter of encouragment to the believers. Phoebe was a lay leader in the church at Cenchrae just outside of Corinth. These 55 short words reveal the portrait of a dependable woman who was dedicated to the cause of Christ.

What do you think Paul meant when he referred to Phoebe as "our sister"?

_____

Do you have friends that are as close to you as your siblings? What makes them special to you? _____

A sister in the Lord is a treasure. She can be someone with whom you share scripture, prayer needs and special concerns. She is the one who loves you just like you are. Someone with whom you can cry and laugh.

Read **Proverbs 18:24**. Write your thoughts on friendship. _____

_____

II. Phoebe - Servant

Phoebe was a servant in the church. How might she have served ? _____

_____

Are there special requirements for being a servant? _____

_____

III. Phoebe - Saint

When does a person become a saint? _____

_____

Are there special requirements for sainthood? Can a person be a saint and not act saintly? _____

Read and write your thoughts:

> **Romans 1:7**
> **I Corinthians 1:2**
> **Psalm 16:3**

Do you consider yourself a saint? _____

IV. Phoebe - Succourer

The term "succourer" is a classic Greek word describing someone who "stands by in case of need". Phoebe probably had to step forward, speak up and show strength as a new convert of Christ. She most likely dedicated herself to being available to meet any need that came along. She certainly must have been open to support the ministry of Paul and to help in teaching about Jesus.

Those who are available to serve are the backbone of the church. The church was under pressure as every effort was made to disrupt their meetings and bring doubt on the leadership. This put extra work on everyone.

V. Phoebe - Safeguarder

How important to you is dependability? _____

Isn't it comforting when you ask someone to do something and you know you don't have to worry that it will be done? It was important to the new churches to have individuals that were not only consecrated, but dependable.

Phoebe had demonstrated her consecration, dedication and dependability through her involvement in the church in Cenchrea. Paul must have found out that Phoebe was going to make a trip to Rome and asked of her a special favor.

What might Paul have said as he placed in her hand the letter to the Romans?

_____

_____

How do you think Phoebe must have felt to be given the responsibility of safeguarding and delivering the letter to the believers in Rome?

_____

_____

Do you think she read the letter? _____

Do you think she checked periodically to see that the letter was safe? _____

What do you think she said as she hand delivered this priceless gift? _____

_____

The letter to the Romans is one of the greatest books on doctrine in the Bible. You are still reaping the benefit of the letter delivered by Phoebe. Phoebe was **wholly** dedicated and **holy** consecrated. This is a powerful combination when placed into action in the life of a Christian. As a **Woman of Worth**, be reminded that the priceless gift of the message of Jesus is left to you to safeguard and deliver just as Phoebe delivered the letter from Paul to the Romans.

As you end this day, pray about your dedication to growing in Christ. Are you continuing to know more about God every day? Do you hunger for the Word and do you enjoy the friendship of other Christians? End this day with a prayer thanking God for His dependability.

LIVING THE FAST LIFE

Fasting has been practiced throughout Christian history. The life of Jesus is the primary example of the importance of fasting. Many of the church fathers expected their congregations to participate in regular fasts. In Colonial New England an annual fast was practiced. Since the beginning of our nation, there have been times when our leaders have called for a day of prayer and fasting.

Refer back to your notes. What have you learned about fasting?

As you fast and pray today, spend time evaluating your experience. Have you found that you are more sensitive to the presence of God in your life?

Do you feel that fasting has been beneficial to your overall spiritual development?

Would you consider fasting either weekly or monthly and use that day to pray for special needs?

What do you think has been accomplished during this eight week period? Are you further along in your Christian pilgrimage? Has there been something special that you have experienced during these times of prayer? Write your thoughts.

_____

_____

_____

List three goals that you would like to accomplish in your Christian pilgrimage.

1. _____

2. _____

3. _____

In becoming a **Woman of Worth**, you will travel a path that includes both peaks and valleys. God doesn't expect you to race through life, but to walk through each day, facing the challenges with assurance that He is with you. The Holy Spirit of God is the premium blessing given into your life. His presence will meet any need. Only after Jesus returned to heaven did the Holy Spirit reside **in** the life of the believer. Now you have Him in His fullness.

Read **John 8:12.** Do the following exercise.

Close your eyes. Clear your mind. Picture a path. This is the path of life. You can't see the end from here. It is a long and winding path that continues until you enter your eternal home. Walk and look around. What do you see along the way? Can you smell the flowers? How tall are the trees? What sounds do you hear? Can you taste the coolness in the air? Walk on. What colors surround you? Can you see the sky above? Walk!

There appears to be some turns up ahead. Keep walking. It is getting steeper. You stumble. Keep walking. The clouds are gathering. It might rain. The air feels thick. You can't see very well. Keep walking. It is foggy. You are getting tired. Your feet are starting to ache. Your legs seem heavy as stones. You are hungry. You are afraid. There are rocks in the path. Keep walking.

There is a presence! You don't feel tired anymore. The path doesn't seem so steep. The way is getting clear. You are no longer afraid. He is guiding you along through the fog. He is reassuring you that you will make it. He says "Focus on the light! Continue to walk!" He says "You are part of a wonderful plan. God's plan." This presence is the Holy Spirit.

You can trust His presence and power along the path of life.

The question is not can you trust God along this path, but will you trust Him?

What challenge are you facing? _____

Do you confidently know that God has already prepared the answer? Write a scripture that you will memorize to encourage you to remain steady?

End this day by thanking God for the Holy Spirit.

Observations Regarding Consecration

A person dedicated to Jesus cannot be stopped from sharing. As the gospel spread, thousands were coming to Christ. Tabitha and Phoebe were two women who, after hearing about Jesus, were totally sold out. Consecrated. Dedicated.

Read **Acts 5:14**. Write your thoughts. _____

_____

Tabitha and Phoebe were contagious Christians!

Do you know someone who is a contagious Christian?_____

A consecrated person is always willing to share.
A consecrated person will create opportunities to tell about Jesus.
A consecrated person has an excitement that is contagious.

The dedication of the women of the New Testament church was one reason the gospel rapidly spread.

Lay leadership is essential in maintaining the growth of the church.

There are multitudes of different "tools" that can be used in witnessing.

The personal testimony of Tabitha and Phoebe resulted in salvation.

The churches were strengthened because these women were involved.

The church is not a building. It is people. It is you!

Read **Acts 5:42**. Write your thoughts. _____

_____

Why do you think God chose to leave the responsibility of spreading the message of Jesus up to individuals? _____

_____

What do you think Tabitha and Phoebe said about Jesus? _____

_____

No one can argue or debate a personal testimony, because it is personal!

Write your personal testimony. Include in your testimony, what your life was like before Jesus, how you came to know Jesus and how your life is different since coming to know Jesus. _____

_____

_____

_____

_____

_____

There is no set pattern for witnessing.

Pray and expect God to open up a window of opportunity for you to share. At first you may feel afraid or unsure. The more often you share your faith, the more comfortable you will become. Your personal testimony should be fresh because of what Jesus is doing in your life every day.

Be available.
Be sensitive.
Be determined.

End this day by making a commitment to share your faith this week.

Personal Applications - Consecration

The path to becoming a **Woman of Worth** is a path directed by God.

The women that were selected for this study are representative of millions of women who have decided to faithfully trust God. Your worth as a woman is determined **first** by your relationship with God. Each of these women are just like you. They had jobs, families and homes. They faced the same type of challenges that you face. By their dedication and faith, they worked through the problems of discouragement, conflict, dissapointment, grief, depression and anxiety. Each woman came to the conclusion that beginning a relationship with God was the starting point to building her self worth. As is seen from the personal stories of these women, each one became a women of confidence, maturity, and loveliness. Every one of these women became a **Woman of Worth.**

List eight aspects of **<u>Becoming a Woman of Worth</u>** that you have studied.

1. **The Woman of Samaria** - She came to understand that a commitment to Jesus will change your life.

Write a thought about commitment. _____

_____

2. **Esther** - She reigned as queen, but rescued a nation.

Write a thought about wisdom. _____

_____

3. **Mary Magdalene** - She went from being submitted to Satan to being submitted to the Savior.

Write a thought about submission. _____

_____

4. Hannah - She was delivered from the depths of depression.

Write a thought about having victory. _____

_____

5. Martha - She opened her heart and her home to Jesus.

6. Mary - She anointed Him with fragrant perfume. He anointed Her with the fragrance of His life.

Write a thought about devotion. _____

_____

7. Deborah - She was a leader who was steady, with courage and ready with boldness.

Write a thought about leadership. _____

_____

8. Tabitha - She used her needle as a witnessing tool.

9. Phoebe - She carried a letter in her hand and a message on her heart.

Write a thought about consecration. _____

_____

Which of these women has been the most interesting to you? Write your thoughts. _____

_____

_____

In preparing the material for this study and in learning about the women of ancient Bible times, I learned about myself. It encouraged me to think that every woman, at some time, has to deal with the a lack of self confidence. I took time to examine the weaknesses and strengths of each woman. I then looked at how God revealed Himself to them and how He unfolded His plan for their unique personalities. I then thought about my life and God's plan for me.

I asked myself the question, "Am I important to the Kingdom Plan of God, too? Can God use me in some way?"

I am just a wife and mother with a job and responsibilities that sometimes don't seem very important. Through the eyes of the women of the Bible, I found that some things never change. We all have to deal with issues regarding self worth and how to develop our personality and style. We all have to come to decide that we are indeed important to the plan that God has for our lives.

My prayer for you is that you will see that only you can fulfill the task that God has for you. Just as the women of the Bible influence us with their lives, you will influence generations yet unborn. You can be the legacy of faith to whom women of the future look for continued encouragment and strength. Your weaknesses and strengths can help other women to become **Women of Worth.**

I will pray that you will allow God to lead you to become all that He has planned. I hope you will know how important you are and when you find yourself with deflated self worth and bashed confidence, you will return in faith to God. He will lift you back to the heights of confidence and will reassure you that you are indeed a **Woman of Worth**.

Becky Drace

A prayer to end the week: Oh Lord, help me to face each day in Your strength and confidence. I praise You for Your plan for my life. I pray for the future generations of women. Help me to remember that You have chosen me to spread Your love to those under my influence. Help me to treasure Your Word and to look for opportunities to share Your message. When I am discouraged, help me to come to You. Thank You that You are always available to me.

I love You, Lord!

Becoming
a
Woman of Worth

TEACHING GUIDE
for
Small Group Study

TEACHING GUIDE FOR SMALL GROUP STUDY

Each group should have no more than 12 members.

Prepare yourself spiritually for the introductory session. Pray that God will lead women who need to develop a more intimate relationship with Him to come to this session. Begin your journal and ask each member to bring their journal next week.

Have materials available including the study book, extra paper and pencils.

Be sensitive and prepared to answer questions regarding the day of fast. The fast will be from after the evening meal on day # 2 until the evening meal on day #3.

Some questions which might be asked:

1. Can I take the class and not fast because I have a medical condition? Yes. It is wise to check with a physician if there are dietary problems. If fasting is not possible, then suggest that they fast from something other than food. Perhaps no telephone calls or television for the 24 hour period. Let them select something that is as important to them as food.
2. Will I get hungry? Yes.
3. Can I drink liquids? Yes, drink juice or clear beverages.

The class is an eight week study of nine women in the Bible. Each student will be responsible to keep up her homework daily. Be available to help any student who gets behind. **The goal is to begin as a group and finish as a group.**

Explain to each member about keeping a journal for their thoughts and questions that might arise. These will be discussed in the group session.

As the group leader, pray about each of your members and then pair them into groups of two. These will become prayer partners during the eight weeks. Encourage them to contact each other at least once each week for support.

SMALL GROUP GUIDE - WEEK ONE
TRANSFORMED

This session will cover the topic of being transformed into a **Woman of Worth.** You will review what it means to be chosen by God, changed to be like Him, and called by Him for His Kingdom Plan. Remember you are to follow the guide, but be adaptable as the Holy Spirit leads each session. Ask for members to share and if they are a little hesitant, call on one. Be sensitive not to embarrass a student. The goal is to become a **sharing - caring** group.

PRAYER TIME - (15 minutes)

Give members time to mention their prayer requests. Tell them to write them down in their journal so they can pray during the week.

LESSON REVIEW - Group discussion - (40 minutes)

A Woman of Worth is a woman being transformed.

Review memory verse - **Romans 12:2.** Ask a student to quote this verse.

Transformation is a process. Review this principle for the week.
What does the word metamorphosis mean to you?

Have a student read **II Corinthians 5:17.** Discuss how it is possible to put the past behind you and become a new creature in Christ.

Discuss the day of fasting.
Ask for comments regarding the first day spent fasting?
Did you get hungry?
How did you react to the hunger?
What scripture did you use to encourage you?
What impact did this have on your spiritual focus?
Were you more aware of the presence of the Holy Spirit?

Applying the principle. Let students respond to these questions.

When did you know that you were special to God?
Do you have a good self image? If not, do you know why?

Stop and pray with any student who is struggling with self worth.

Ask students to share their responses to these questions.

Do you think you know what God has planned for your life at this time?
Would you be willing to change what you are doing in life if you felt God was moving you in a different direction?

Ask the question. What was the most meaningful part of Week # 1 to you?

Finish this lesson review with the three statements on page 16 which begin with....

"You must trust that God's Word is true......"
"You must be willing to obey His Word...."
"You must be willing to make ...."

INTRODUCTION OF UPCOMING WEEK - (5 minutes)

Next week you will study the life of the Samaritan woman and the commitment she made and how her life was changed.

During the day of fast, you will study the reasons for fasting and how it combines with prayer to bring you into a deeper communion with God.

CLOSING PRAYER - Ask for a student volunteer to close in prayer. Be prepared to close in prayer if a student doesn't volunteer.

Note to leader: As you study to prepare for the group session, ask the Lord to bring to mind any student who needs special prayer. Remember that as a group leader, you may have to spend additional time to encourage a student. God will honor your efforts. Your goal is to encourage your students to reach a new level in their Christian faith.

SMALL GROUP GUIDE - WEEK TWO
COMMITTED

This session will cover the topic of commitment.

PRAYER TIME - (15 minutes)

Give members time to mention their prayer requests. Tell them to write them down in their journal so they can pray during the week.

LESSON REVIEW - Group discussion - (40 minutes)

A Woman of Worth is a woman who makes a commitment to Christ.
Ask for a volunteer to give a brief review of the life of the Samaritan woman.

Review memory verse - **John 4:14.** Ask a student to quote this verse.
Review the principle of commitment. Commitment begins with faith. See page 21.

Have a student read Hebrews 11:6 and discuss the definition of faith and why it pleases God. *Note:* Faith is the basic element of salvation.

Ask your students to share some commitment they have made. For example: piano lessons, a sport, a class, job, special project. What benefits were gained from this experience?

Ask students to share their answers to these questions.

1. Have you ever made a commitment that took more time and energy than you anticipated? What did you do? What level of commitment did the Samaritan woman
make? How can a commitment change your life?
2. Why was the woman of Samaria avoiding contact? Have you ever wanted to be alone? Refer to page 22.

3. How did Jesus offer her hope? Refer to page 24.
4. How had the conditions of the Samaritan woman's life depleted her self esteem and confidence?
5. What is the symbol of the living water? Read John 7:37-39. Remind the group that the Holy Spirit is always available to meet the needs of their life. In what area of life is the need greatest for the Holy Spirit? This will differ with each student.   Drink deeply from the well spring of living water to experience the fullness and confidence of Christ.
6. How can religion become a substitute for a relationship with Christ?

Share about the day spent in fasting.

Have your students share the following.

What is the difference in belief "in" God and being intimate "with" God? Page 28.
Where do you go for solitude? Refer to page 31.
What were your thoughts on Psalm 104?

Finish this lesson review by sharing responses to these questions? Page 35-37.

Did you identify areas where you waste time? What adjustments need to be made in your managing of time?
Did you identify areas where you need clarity?
How have worldly ideas invaded our culture? Your home? What can be done to change your focus?

INTRODUCTION OF UPCOMING WEEK - (5 minutes)

Next week you will study the life of Esther.
As you fast, you will study God's specific and directive will.

CLOSING PRAYER - Ask for a student volunteer to close in prayer. Be prepared to close in prayer if a student doesn't volunteer.

Note to leader: Help the students to understand commitment. Any commitment needs to be taken seriously. To grow a mature intimate relationship with Christ takes a daily commitment. This requires time and energy. As a person commits their lives to Christ, He strengthens them to handle the issues of life.

SMALL GROUP GUIDE - WEEK THREE
WISE

This session will cover the topic of **wisdom.** We need wisdom to meet the demands of family, job and schedules. Can you know if the decisions you are making are the right ones? How are they going to effect the people around you?

Some of your students may be struggling with the difference between knowledge and wisdom. The goal of the lesson is to establish the difference between knowledge and wisdom and how wisdom can help build self worth and confidence.

PRAYER TIME - (15 minutes)

Give members time to update their requests. Remind them to keep their journal current.

LESSON REVIEW - Group discussion - (40 minutes)

A Woman of Worth is a wise woman.

Ask for a volunteer to briefly share the life story of Esther.

Review memory verse - **I Timothy 4:12.** Ask someone to quote this verse.

Review the principle for the week by sharing these questions.

Have someone share the difference between knowledge and wisdom. How does one become wise?
Does age play a part in wisdom?
What decisions have you made that you are sure were wise decisions?
What do you think about the biblical concept of adoption?
What most impressed you about Esther?

160

During the day of fasting, what did you learn from the study of God's specific will and God's directive will? What is the difference?

Have you been praying for a particular individual to be saved?

What are some ways that you can pray for salvation?

Can you compare simply knowing about God and knowing God intimately?

Refer to page 52 and let a student share regarding the questions.

Ask someone to share their written prayer from page 54.

Finish the lesson review by emphasizing that wisdom is given by God and has to be sought on a daily basis. It does not come automatically when you become a believer. Ask - What was the most meaningful part of this week to you?

INTRODUCTION OF UPCOMING WEEK - (5 minutes)

Next week you will study the life of Mary Magdalene and how she submitted in repentance and respect to Jesus Christ. Her life was changed and she was healed.

On the day of fasting, you will study one of the hindrances to a powerful prayer life. Prayer is our communing with God. Communing is a joint venture.

CLOSING PRAYER - Ask for a student to close in prayer.

Note to leader: Get to know your students and encourage friendships to grow. Your goal as a small group leader is to help each student to weekly sense their personal spiritual growth.

SMALL GROUP GUIDE - WEEK FOUR
SUBMISSIVE

This session will cover the topic of submission. Mary Magdalene developed into a **Woman of Worth** first by becoming submissive to the Lord Jesus Christ. Many things will distract you from developing a relationship with Jesus, however, only when you are willing to daily submit to the authority, mercy and forgiveness to God through Jesus will your life become stable and directed. Mental and emotional illness can be devastating. Depression and instability can render you ineffective in your daily Christian life and also keep you from being a witness for Christ.

Your goal in small group will be to understand the necessity of being submitted to Christ so that you will grow in your faith and service to the Lord.

PRAYER TIME - (15 minutes)

Ask for updates on prayer concerns and add any new requests. Split into pairs for a time of prayer for each other.

LESSON REVIEW - (40 minutes)

A Woman of Worth is a woman submitted to daily walk with Jesus Christ.

Ask for a volunteer to give a brief overview of the life of Mary Magdalene.

Review the memory verse - **John 14:21.** Have someone quote the verse.

Discuss the contrast between how our society defines submission and the biblical definition of submission. How is it considered a negative word? In reality it is a positive word when one submits to the authority of God.

How has the term "authority" been misused in our society? Mental, emotional and physical abuse are sometimes the result of misused authority and submission.

Ask your students to read their responses to the questions on page 66 and then comment on these questions.

1. Have you known individuals who have been miraculously healed?
2. Jesus is the light of the world, but said that you are the light of the world? How?
3. How active do you think Satan is? How does he attempt to draw you away from Jesus?
4. What type of evidence should be reflective from the life of a person who is daily walking with Christ? Why do people sometimes return to the pre-Christ life? How can you avoid this temptation and maintain a steady commitment to Jesus?
5. What is so important about the empty tomb? Remember that all other religions do not have a risen Lord!
6. Do you believe in spiritual warfare? Refer to page 71 for a discussion on spiritual warfare. Refer to the protection available to Christians in the battle against Satan. Ephesians 6:10-18.

As you spent the day fasting, did God bring to mind any area which may be unpleasant to Him and be causing a barrier to your prayer life? There are consequences to sinful behavior one of which is that it will stunt the growth in your relationship with Christ and your prayer life will seem shallow.

Review the list on page 72 and discuss any areas of concern.

How do you intend to keep your prayer life fresh and exciting? Does your prayer journal aide you in this? Stop and have a prayer of praise to God simply for who He is to you. Ask each member to join with one statement regarding the nature of God. Confession reaps results!

INTRODUCTION OF UPCOMING WEEK - (5 minutes)

Next week you will study the life of Hannah.
As you fast you will study thanksgiving and its link to prayer.

CLOSING PRAYER - Ask for a student volunteer.

Note to leader: Be sensitive to the subject of submission in helping your group define the term in a biblical way. Also help your group see the need to be thankful and how to find something to be thankful for in all situation.

163

In this session you will study how to have victory over any obstacle. Hannah has been the example of prayer and faith throughout biblical history. However, before she became a role model for all women, she had to deal with issues which would place any normal woman under overwhelming stress.

PRAYER TIME - (15 minutes)

Have students share any areas which need to have group prayer. This is a time to encourage and undergird each other in faith and prayer.

LESSON REVIEW - (40 minutes)

A Woman of Worth is a woman who is victorious over any difficult situation.

Ask for someone to share a brief overview of the life of Hannah.
Review the memory verse - **I Samuel 2:1.** Ask for a volunteer to quote the verse. Review the principle of being victorious. What situations would you consider crisis situations which require spiritual strength in order to have victory? For example: loss of work, death, illness, rebellion, depression.....

Ask your group to share any difficulty they have had with depression. How did Hannah handle her depression in the beginning and then what did she discover about God and herself in the process of maturing into a **Woman of Worth**?

List the areas which were causing Hannah problems. Can you relate? What were the steps toward the recovery and victory in Hannah's life? Review pages 68-71 for seven keys to having victory in any of life's situations.

How does our society deal with problems? Contrast this answer with the above steps in finding victory according to the example of Hannah.

On page 79 there is a question regarding marriage relationships. Help your students to know that ex-spouses and children can find strength and direction from God whenever there is division, hurt, and anger. Divorce is an extremely difficult situation. Some of your students may still have issues relating to separation and divorce or their children may still be hurting from these areas. Your sensitivity can help them to release these areas into the hands of God. See page 86-87...

Release brings peace.

Share about your fasting day. Is it hard to remain thankful in all things? Share responses on page 83.

How did the appearance of Hannah change? Can people tell when you are experiencing some difficulty? Does thanksgiving change your attitude?

How significant was the praise prayer of Hannah in changing her attitude? Read I Samuel 2:1-10

INTRODUCTION OF UPCOMING WEEK - (5 minutes)

You will study the life of Martha and Mary.

During the day of fasting you will examine love and sex and their relationship to prayer.

CLOSING PRAYER - Share one sentence statements of thanksgiving.

Note to leader: When closing the group time, lead your students to understand that situations:

       Sometimes do not change.... I Samuel 2:1

Peninnah continued to be an adversary to Hannah.

       Sometimes are altered.... I Samuel 2:12

Hannah fulfilled her vow to place Samuel in the temple knowing the sons of Eli were corrupt and that the environment might not be healthy.

       Sometimes change ..... I Samuel 2:21

Hannah had several other children besides Samuel. Her womb was blessed.

When we trust God with **ALL** life's challenges, He will give us victory and strength to deal with every new situation which will arise.

The focus on this lesson is on devotion. Out of a heart of devotion will come a desire to give and serve. The strength of the body of Christ is its diversity. Different personalities and abilities can be used individually or come together to reach people with the message of the love of Jesus.

PRAYER TIME - (15 minutes)

Share any new requests or experiences. Ask: Is your prayer time changing?

LESSON REVIEW - (40 minutes)

A Woman of Worth expresses her devotion through love and service.

Have someone share the overview of the family of Martha, Lazarus and Mary.

Review the memory verse - **I Corinthians 12:4-6.** Have someone quote the verse.

Review the principle of devotion. Devotion is a result of a growing relationship. A family devoted to each other can become an instrument that God can use to influence other families. There is no perfect family, but God uses imperfect family members to reveal how He can bring unity from disunity and contentment from chaos.
God wants your family to be loving, emotionally strong and secure.

Share responses to these questions.

1. What is God's desire for a family?
2. What are some of the differences in the personalities of your family members?
3. How do you handle tension in your home?
4. What can you do to help your family become strong in the Lord?
5. What was the difference between the way Martha and Mary expressed their devotion to Jesus? How do you express your devotion to the Lord?
6. Would you consider your life content?

If you could write an epilogue to the story of Martha and Mary, what would it be?

Refer to pages 98-104 and share your responses to the questions.

Share your thoughts on the topic for the day of fasting. What aspects of true love did you find in I Corinthians 13? Will these make a difference in the way you perceive love and sex?

Love is the very essence of all of life. It is the beginning point of God's deepest desire for you. Quote John 3:16 and share what this verse means to you.

Your attitude toward love and sex determines the extent of your ability to experience fulfillment in this area. Many relationship problems begin with perceptions regarding love and sex.

Did you identify where God needs to change your attitude or heal a hurt in this area?
Purity in your sex life is essential to your daily walk of faith. Our society tries desperately to redefine sex, and what is acceptable sexual behavior, however, God's word is clear.

INTRODUCTION OF UPCOMING WEEK - (5 minutes)

Next week you will study the life of Deborah and the controversial area of women in leadership. Be prayerful as you prepare.

Through fasting and prayer doubt can be eliminated. You will look at doubt as a hindrance to a powerful prayer life.

CLOSING PRAYER - Have a prayer time involving as many of the group as will pray for each other. We need to be persistent in praying for each other.

Note to leader: Be ultra sensitive in the discussion of sex. God's word is clear and His desire is for a life of fulfillment and satisfaction. Help move your students into an attitude of acceptance of sex as a beautiful part of God's overall plan for life. Ask for a commitment of each student to a life of sexual purity in and out of marriage.

```
┌─────────────────────────────────────────┐
│     SMALL GROUP GUIDE - WEEK  SEVEN      │
│                 LEADER                   │
└─────────────────────────────────────────┘
```

This session will concentrate on leadership and authority. The life of Deborah will reveal how God called her and how she responded to be used to lead and restore the Israelites. Because of the strength and courage of Deborah, Israel was at peace for 40 years.

PRAYER TIME - (15 minutes)

Give members time to share any experience during this week. Have them refer to their journals to refresh their memories.

LESSON REVIEW - (40 minutes)

A Woman of Worth knows her strength, who is in authority and how to be an effective leader.

Ask someone to share a recap of the life of Deborah.
Review the memory verse - **Deuteronomy 31:6**. Ask someone to quote the verse.
Review the principle of leadership. Being an effective leader requires boldness and courage.

Use yourself as an example and have the other group members identify your leadership qualities. Do this for each group member. Sometimes it is difficult to identify your own strengths and abilities.

Refer to page 120. Which woman made the greatest impression of leadership? Have your group members share their responses to the questions regarding their role models.

What is the contrast between the way women are viewed today and in Deborah's day?
Is it easier to be a woman leader or not?

Refer to the questions on page 121-125 and ask for someone to share their views on marriage, leadership and authority.

Have someone read Judges 4: 6-7. Do you think Barak had weak faith?

Have you ever declared victory before the battle was over? Ask for someone to share how important strong faith is in the battles of life?

How do you determine which battles are worth fighting? Remind your students to pick their battles wisely. You can't fight every battle, but when God's word is in question, then the issues must be addressed.

How do leading and following compliment each other?

Ask for someone to share about the topic of fasting - doubt. What causes doubt? How can you deal with frequent doubt? See page 127.

Where do you see that you could become a leader? How can you use this position to be a witness for Christ?

Review the five leadership principles and five leadership characteristics on page 130. Finish the lesson review by asking someone to share their poem on page 125.

INTRODUCTION OF UPCOMING WEEK - (5 minutes)

Next week will the the last week of this study. You will study the lives of Tabitha and Phoebe. You will study contagious Christianity. Issue a challenge to share their faith with at least one person this next week.

Your day of fasting will focus on your experience in this unique discipline.

CLOSING PRAYER - Ask someone to pray that God will raise up leaders.

Note to leader: The ammunition for the battles of life is the sword of the Lord - the Word of God. You must be prepared before you go to battle. If you are to become a strong leader to defend your faith and your family, then you must study daily what God's word says. Help your students identify that a sensitive leader is a successful leader.

This week is the last week of this series of studies on **Becoming a Woman of Worth.** You will study the excitement of being a contagious Christian. That is one who uses their position in life: student, friend, neighbor, fellow employee, as an opportunity to share about their personal relationship with Jesus Christ. To be consecrated is to be dedicated.

PRAYER TIME - (15 minutes)

As you pray for the last time as a group, share requests, answers to prayer or other praises. Have a prayer of thanksgiving for friendship.

LESSON REVIEW - (40 minutes)

A Woman of Worth is a consecrated woman, dedicated to growing in holiness and being faithful to share her faith in Christ.

Ask one person to share an overview of the life of Tabitha and someone else to share the life of Phoebe.

Review the memory verse - **I Thessalonians 5:23**. Ask someone to quote the verse.
Review the principle of consecration. Living a holy life requires diligence. Only God is holy but He has said that we can lead a life of holiness.

You are special to God and He loves you.

How can you be a holy woman when you are surrounded by unholiness?

How has your life changed since you became a Christian? How would a stranger know that you are a believer in Jesus Christ?

How did the lives of Tabitha and Phoebe effect their acquaintances?

170

Would you classify yourself as a disciple of Christ? Is your life filled with good works? What is your response to the question: "Are you a saint?"

What was Dorcas' trade? How did she influence her surroundings? What is your trade? Can you develop a plan for using your trade as a tool to share your personal faith?

What do you think Phoebe thought when Paul asked her to deliver the letter to the believers in Rome? Have you ever been given a particular responsibility and felt very honored to fulfill the request?

Who do you consider your very best friends? Do they encourage you to reach your potential for Christ? How do you encourage them?

Refer to page 150-151. Using these nine women as patterns, do you plan to make any changes in your life or any new commitments in the way you serve the Lord?

Which woman has been the greatest inspiration to you? Which one of the lessons do you think needs the most attention in your life?

How will you integrate fasting into your spiritual walk?

What three goals did you list on page 146?

What one challenge did you list on page 147?

CLOSING PRAYER - Use this time as a time of dedication and commitment. Pray around the circle having each lady pray for the person on their right. As you bring this time to an end, assure your group that you will continue to be available to help them with any area of need and to continue to pray with them.

Note to leader: You might suggest that the group continue to meet with their prayer accountability partner for encouragement.

One of the greatest experiences of my Christian pilgrimage is the women that have been my prayer partners, mentors and friends.

EIGHT PRINCIPLES ON BECOMING A WOMAN OF WORTH

Willing to be transformed into the image of Jesus Christ.

Willing to be committed to a personal relationship with Jesus.

Willing to seek the wisdom of God in every situation of life.

Willing to submit to the authority of God to guide your life.

Willing to claim victory before the battle is fought.

Willing to devote your home to the presence of Christ.

Willing to become a leader under the guidance of God.

Willing to consecrate your vocation and life's activities as a tool for sharing the gospel of Jesus Christ.

HELPS FOR A POWERFUL PRAYER LIFE

Begin every prayer time with a prayer of praise for who God is in your life. "You, Oh God, are Holy, Supreme, Merciful", etc. Study the characteristics of God.

Read scripture to help you focus totally on the presence of God.

Ask God to reveal where you have been unpleasant to Him. Is there sin in your life that you must first acknowledge before your relationship with God is pure? Ask the Holy Spirit for a clear picture of your life as God sees it.

Examine areas of weakness and reinforce these areas with scripture for strength. For example:

> Do you have doubt?
> Are there unresolved issues in relationships?
> Are you harboring anger or bitterness?
> Are you a selfish person?
> Do you pass blame?
> Are you negligent to help a less fortunate person?
> Are you disobedient or rebellious?

> Refer to page 66 as a reminder of other possible areas of need.

Have a time of thanksgiving where you offer your gratitude to God for what He is doing in your life.

Claim that a glorious work is being done in your life.

Organize your requests into groups for better focus during your prayer time.

Keep a daily journal of your prayer requests and answers to prayer.

Close your time of prayer with a time of praise.

THE AMMUNITION FOR BATTLE
EPHESIANS 6:10-17

All of the battles of life have already been fought and won by Jesus. The victory is already yours, however, you daily must faithfully confront the ongoing attack by Satan to defeat you in your Christian walk. Satan wants you to believe that Jesus has left you vulnerable and weak.

As a believer your eternal destiny is sealed, but each day you have to face situations which require a direct confrontation. Some of the battles are severe, some are subtle. Either one is Satan's attempt to distract and discourage you in order to render you ineffective as a personal witness for Jesus.

If Satan can keep you mute and afraid to share your faith, then he has won the battle of the day!

You have equipment to sustain you. It is wise to memorize passages to help you be prepared to face any challenge which comes along.

Ephesians 6:10 - Your strength is in the Lord! He is powerful and mighty!
Ephesians 6: 13 - Put on your armor! Stand up and face the enemy!
Ephesians 6:14 - Wrap your waist with the belt of truth!
Ephesians 6:14 - Protect your breast with righteousness!
Ephesians 6:15 - Place on your feet the gospel of peace!
Ephesians 6:16 - Carry before you the shield of faith!
Ephesians 6:17 - Protect your mind with the assurance of salvation!
Ephesians 6:17 - Use the sword of the Spirit! The Word is powerful!

Throughout the life of Jesus, we see that He daily communed with His father for strength to endure and defeat any negative comment or difficult situation.

Victory will come when you experience the peace of knowing that your life is being held carefully and tenderly by the Holy Supreme creator of all. As you depend on Him for strength, your life will begin to reflect the results of a growing relationship. You will become more content and able to deal with daily occurrences.

Battle equipment has to be checked and maintained regularly. Prayer is the way you maintain your battle equipment.

174

SCRIPTURE FOR WISDOM

Deuteronomy 4:5-6 - "Surely I have taught you statutes and judgments, just as the Lord my God commanded me, that you should act according to them in the land which you go to possess. Therefore be careful to observe them, for this is your wisdom and your understanding in the sight of the peoples who will hear all these statutes and say, 'Surely this great nation is a wise and understanding people'".

Proverbs 3:13 - "Happy is the man who finds wisdom, and the man who gains understanding."

Proverbs 4:7 - "Wisdom is the principle thing, therefore get wisdom, and in all your getting, get understanding."

Proverbs 9:10 - "The fear of the Lord is the beginning of wisdom, and the knowledge of the Holy One is understanding."

Proverbs 16:16 - "How much better it is to get wisdom than gold! and to get understanding rather than silver."

Ecclesiastes 9:17-18a. - "Words of the wise, spoken quietly should be heard rather than the shout of a ruler of fools. Wisdom is better than weapons of war."

I Corinthians 3:18-19 - "Let no one deceive himself. If anyone among you seems to be wise in this age, let him become a fool that he may become wise. For the wisdom of this world is foolishness with God."

Colossians 2: 2b-3 - "...both of the Father and of Christ, in whom are hidden all the treasures of wisdom and knowledge."

Colossians 4:5 - "Walk in wisdom toward those who are outside, redeeming the time. Let your speech always be with grace, seasoned with salt, that you may know how you ought to answer each one."

James 1:5 - "If any of you lacks wisdom, let him ask of God, who gives to all liberally and without reproach and it will be given to him."

SCRIPTURE FOR PRAISE

Psalm 34:1 - "I will bless the Lord at all times, His praise shall continually be in my mouth."

Psalm 67:3 - "Let the peoples praise you, O God; Let all the peoples praise you."

Psalm 69:34 - "Let heaven and earth praise Him, the seas and everything that moves in them."

Psalm 148:1 - "Praise the Lord! Sing to the Lord a new song, and His praise in the congregation of saints."

Psalm 150:6 - "Praise Him with the sound of the trumpet! Praise Him with the lute and harp! Praise Him with the timbrel and dance! Praise Him with stringed instruments and flutes! Praise Him with loud cymbals! Praise Him with clashing cymbals! Let everything that has breath praise the Lord! Praise the Lord!

Hebrews 2:12 - "I will declare Your name to my brethren; in the midst of the congregation, I will sing praise to You."

Hebrews 13:15 - "Therefore by Him let us continually offer the sacrifice of praise to God, that is the fruit of our lips, giving thanks to His name."

Becoming a Woman of Worth

REAL
QUESTIONS
from
REAL
WOMEN

REAL QUESTIONS FROM REAL WOMEN

1. I have been unfaithful to my husband more than once and my past is always hanging over my head. He is so hurt; what can I do?

2. I had an abortion a few years ago. How can I get rid of the guilt and feeling depressed all the time?

3. Why should I only date a believer? Do you really think God has someone special for me to marry?

4. I am married to a man who loves me and our children, but he isn't a Christian. I knew he wasn't a Christian when we married; now what do I do?

5. I feel so depressed most of the time. I get mad and then rant and rave. I am on medication to control my emotions. How can I get a grip?

6. My teenage daughter is sexually active. I am so afraid that she will get pregnant. What can I do?

7. I have this lady that obviously hates me. She treats me awful and I don't know how to love her like the Bible says I should. What do you suggest?

8. I am in college and am so busy. I have a hard time staying consistent in my Bible study and prayer time. What suggestions do you have to help me?

9. My husband has announced that he is gay. Now what do I do?

10. I wasn't raised in a Christian family. I only became a Christian a year ago. How can I be a witness to my family?

I have been unfaithful to my husband more than once and my past is always hanging over my head. He is so hurt; what can I do?

1. If you have been unfaithful you need to ask some pointed questions.

> Why am I not satisfied with my husband?
> What causes me to do things that hurt myself and others?
> What past experiences possibly influence my present actions?
> Do I not feel that I deserve a good marriage and family?

2. Everyone has a past. The wonderful thing is that when we release our past to the Lord, He presents us with the possibility of a new beginning.

3. Consequences are the most difficult part of dealing with behavior. Only God can heal hurt and repair broken relationships. Only He can restore lost love.

2. There are many good helps for strengthening your relationship with your husband. Christian counselors and trained clergy can help you clarify many of the issues you are facing.

3. You must first seek forgiveness from God for the unfaithfulness and hurt that you have brought into your life and the lives of your family.

4. You must faithfully try to restore the trust that has been broken.

5. You will need to have a good accountability person to go to for prayer support and encouragement. This needs to be a woman who is grounded in her faith in Christ and someone who is knowledgeable in scripture.

6. Stay away from any areas of temptation that might entice you.

7. Keep your marriage as the main priority and pray and ASK the Holy Spirit to guide you and restore your husband's love for you.

8. Refuse to allow guilt or discouragement to overtake you.

Proverbs 3:5-6 "Trust in the Lord with all your heart and lean not unto your own understanding. In all your ways acknowledge Him and He will direct your paths."

I had an abortion a few years ago. How can I get rid of the guilt and feeling depressed all the time?

Abortion is common today. Unfortunately many woman do not seek advice as to how to handle the aftermath of abortion.

1. The first step in dealing with any guilt is forgiveness.

You must seek forgiveness from the Lord and then be willing to work through forgiving yourself. When God forgives, He does so completely. He never brings back to your memory the reason for your guilt. That comes from the deceiver, Satan. He knows that if he can infiltrate your thinking that he can keep you from accepting the truths of God's mercy and grace. The bondage of guilt keeps many women from being able to experience the pleasure of God's presence and the peace of His love.

2. You can not undo what has been done, but you can move forward and become a witness of God's love and forgiveness to other women who have had similar experiences. Any experience can be a blessing or a curse. Even the most desperate of situations can be used by God to bring honor and glory to Him, if we are willing to seek Him for direction and healing.

3. There are Christian support groups for women who have had abortions. This can be a source of encouragement to help you when you are reminded of your past.

4. Seek scripture that will lift you in praise and thanksgiving for what God is doing in your life. Praise always is pleasing to the Lord and He uses praise to encourage you. Praise and thanksgiving cannot occupy the same space with guilt.

Grace is offered,
Willingly receive!
Forgiveness is a gift!
Accept the package!

I John 1:9 "If you confess your sin, He is faithful and just to forgive you of your sin and cleanse you from all unrighteousness."
Psalm 103:11-12 "For as the heavens are high above the earth, so great is his mercy toward those who fear Him; As far as the east is from the west, so far has He removed our transgressions from us."

180

Why should I only date a believer? Do you really think God has someone special for me to marry?

I know that God has a plan for your life! He cared enough for you that He prepared a way for you to have a relationship with Him through His son, Jesus Christ. If He loves you this much, then He most certainly wants what is best for your life and that includes the best person for you to share your life with.

If you are a believer, you will find that your common interests are in contrast to the interests of friends who are not believers. Their values and ideals, their standards and goals will be in contrast with you if you are seeking to follow God with your life.

Your closest friendships must be God-centered if you want your life to be honoring to God. Both male and female friendships should be mutually encouraging toward Christ. You should build each other up and continually encourage each other to reach your full potential as a Christian. Non believers will not do that. Non believers do not understand the concepts of the Christian life.

Your only reason to be friends with non-believers is to show them the love of Christ and help them to see their need to know Christ.

God has someone special for you who will compliment you and you will compliment him. Do not settle for what you consider to be a good choice when God wants the person that is best for you.

Criteria for marriage
Marry a man who has a personal relationship with Christ.
Marry a man who seeks God's guidance before he makes decisions.
Marry a man who wants to maintain a God-centered family.
Marry a man who is honest and faithful with his possessions.
Marry a man who is not embarrassed to pray with you and for you.
Marry a man who understands forgiveness.

II Corinthians 6:14 "Do not be unequally yoked together with unbelievers, for what fellowship has righteousness with lawlessness? And what communion has light with darkness?"

181

I am married to a man who loves me and the children, but he isn't a Christian. I knew he wasn't a Christian when we married; now what do I do?

Many women find themselves in this situation. If your husband loves you and is a good father and provider, you have been blessed. If you have limited conflict in your household, again you are blessed.

1. Claim salvation for your household. - II Peter 3:9
   God's greatest desire is that your family be united under Him.

2. Be consistent and faithful to pray for the salvation of your husband.
   Every day you must pray that God will encircle your husband with His presence and bring some spiritual influence into his daily activities.

3. Seek guidance from the Lord in how you can be a sweet witness and not become a stumbling block by nagging or belittling your husband.
   Some women fall victim to becoming their own worst enemy in seeing their husband become a Christian.

4. Be faithful in your own personal growth as a Christian.
   If you are not faithful and consistent in your daily life, then you are not providing an example to follow. Our walk is more important than our talk.

5. Find ways to be thankful for your husband and to express your love and appreciation to him. A negative attitude is destructive.

6. Be understanding when your husband disagrees with you on spiritual matters. Remember that as an unbeliever, his heart is bound in unbelief and his spiritual eyes are covered to understanding the things of God. He will not see things as you do. You will need to be sensitive and tender if you want to see him respond.

You need to realize that your husband has to come to acceptance of Christ on his own. Many women have seen husbands saved after years of faithfully praying and consistently living as a witness to their husbands.
I Peter 3:1 "Likewise, you wives, be submissive to your own husbands, that even if some do not obey the word, they, without a word, may be won by the conduct of their wives, when they observe your chaste conduct accompanied by fear (respect)."

My teenager is sexually active. I am so afraid that she will get pregnant. What can I do?

Many parents live in fear of unwanted pregnancy. There is incredible pressure on our children to become sexually involved. Television and movies create a false definition of love and intimacy and we constantly must battle the humanistic viewpoint on these issues. Abortion is common as a means of birth control.

If your child is not sexually active, reinforce to them regularly that staying pure sexually until they marry is God's best plan for them. Sex is for marriage and is part of God's covenant to families. They need to know that you understand the pressure that they are under.

Your child needs to understand that guilt and hurt are the results of impurity and once virginity is gone it can never again be regained. Only forgiveness can be experienced.

Tell your child that you are daily praying about the sexual pressure that they are experiencing. Let them hear you pray for them about this area.

If your child is sexually active, you must let them know that you are aware of their activity. You must talk with them about the possible consequences of their actions and how this will influence any future plans they might have. Be direct and frank, but loving and tender. Be available to your child; communication is vital.

Birth control pills and abortion are not the answer to the problem of sexual activity. It might relieve you as a parent from having to deal with pregnancy, but the standards that are communicated are in direct contrast to what God intends.

You need to think about the decisions which will have to be made should pregnancy occur.

God's wisdom is needed when dealing with teenage pressures. As a parent we are not guaranteed that our children will respect our values, but we are assured that God will give us wisdom and courage when it is needed.

I Thessalonians 4:3 " This is the will of God, your sanctification; that you should abstain from sexual immorality."

183

I feel so depressed most of the time. I get mad and then rant and rave. I am on medication to control my emotions. How can I get a grip?

There is help available in dealing with emotions which have spiraled out of control. Sometimes it is difficult to determine the origin of emotional difficulties. One of the most frequent topics of discussion in women's groups is how to deal with depression.

1. Is your depression a result of a medical situation which needs attention? Perhaps an appointment with a trusted physician is needed. Most women experience bouts of "blue days" but frequent depression must be addressed.

2. Is your behavior a result of unresolved conflict? Perhaps you have left some area of your life unattended that you need to resolve before you can see a change in your emotional state. A frank examination is sometimes necessary.

3. Expressing anger with rage is unhealthy for you and those that are in the path of your raving. You can see miraculous results if you are willing to seek God's word for scripture that will help to calm you when you sense that your anger is rising.

4. Depression is not of God. He wants your life to be experienced in the abundance of His goodness, but it is up to you if you are willing to diligently pursue His presence to help you in dealing with emotions which are out of control.

5. Your goal as a Christian should be to have a life that is filled with praise and thanksgiving. It is hard to be depressed when your heart is expressing gratitude. Many verses in the book of Psalm can help you replace negative emotions by refocusing on gratitude for God's goodness instead of your despair.

6. An accountability partner who will be honest with you and help you pray about your depression and anger could be a positive step toward emotional health.

Psalm 42:11 "Why are you cast down, Oh my soul? And why are you disquieted within me? Hope in God. For I shall yet praise Him, the help of my countenance and my God."

I have this lady that obviously hates me. She treats me awful and I don't know how to love her like the Bible says I should. What do you suggest?

Dislike can cause such pain. You can receive hundreds of positive comments only to have them dashed by one act of disapproval.

1. Be certain that you haven't offended this person in some way. If you determine that you have offended her by something you have done or said, you will need to apologize. If this doesn't resolve the conflict, then there is something else that is taking place to cause her behavior.

2. Try to be pleasant and hospitable to her when you are in her presence.

3. Only God can love some people. You and I are unable to love completely as God loves because we are so influenced by human emotions and actions. However, we can express grace to any person by asking God to let you view them as He does. He sees who a person can become, not who they are.

4. Remind yourself that the individual probably doesn't hate you. It is most likely something that you represent. Perhaps they envy your family relationship, your home, your reputation, your looks, your money. Maybe they envy the fact that you are respected among your peers. Maybe they are just unhappy and don't like you because you are a joyful person.

5. If you have tried to be a friend, then you are released from their continuing hatefulness. Pray for the individual but do not allow this to consume your thinking.

6. Do not talk about this with other friends. Gossip will cause more problems than the hateful behavior. The only exception to this is to ask your prayer partner to pray for you in wisdom to deal with this situation.

Romans 12:21 "Do be overcome by evil, but overcome evil with good."

I am in college and am so busy. I have a hard time staying consistent in my Bible study and prayer time. What suggestions do you have to help me?

All of us have busy schedules. Prioritizing our time is necessary if we are going to be productive. Have you ever wondered how some people seem to get so much done and others are so disorganized and unproductive?

As a believer, your greatest source of strength to meet the challenges of college life is in your personal relationship with God through His son, Jesus. God can do more with your 24 hour day than you could ever begin to imagine.

You must set the course of your day by spending time in His word. One verse from the book of Psalm or Proverbs will begin your day with a positive approach. Starting the day with praise sets the beginning tone, then set aside some time to spend in prayer before the day ends. Be careful not to wait until all your energy has been spent on college activities before you decide to spend time with the Lord.

1. Take time to evaluate your priorities. What do you spend most of your time doing? Do you have a job? How many hours are you taking and how much preparation does this require? Can you rearrange some of your activities? Evaluation of your priorities needs to be done on a regular basis, at least once each semester.

2. Are you spending too much time on relationships? Relationships are important, but can consume much time and energy. You need to be selective in your relationship development.

3. Are you spending too much time focusing on grades? You are in college for two reasons, to grow academically in your field and to grow as a Christian. Both of these are vital to your development as the person God wants you to become. When you are out of balance in any area it is time to reconsider your priorities.

We all have one thing in common. Every day has 24 hours.

Psalm 90:12 "So teach us to number our days, that we may gain a heart of wisdom."

186

My husband has announced that he is gay. Now what do I do?

Homosexuality has become a major issue in our society. Families are upended when someone "comes out of the closet".

Any sinful behavior has consequences that cause damage and pain, but the issue of homosexuality has problems which are peculiar to this lifestyle. Children are especially vulnerable to the difficulties brought on by homosexual choices.

The debate over whether a person is born homosexual has not been settled. God's word addresses homosexuality. From the beginning, God did not establish homosexuality as a normal alternative life style for families.

1. Consideration should be taken as to how you will explain this to your children.

2. The Aids issue must be considered.

3. The emotions of anger, confusion, rejection, hurt, rage, and bitterness must be handled as they arise.

4. A wise clergyman or counselor or a trusted friend may be needed to help you make plans for your future. Tough love must be practiced, but grace expressed.

The choice that your husband has made leaves you with the responsibility of making sense from the senseless. You now have to work through all your thoughts and feelings and will need to retain as normal a life as possible.

5. Your church family will be important and a small close circle of friends to support and undergird you will be necessary.

6. Only God can bring back the person who has selected to reject Him and ultimately this is rejection of God. You and your family are the ones who have to deal with the issues that homosexuality presents.

7. Prayer and God's power can sustain you, but there are no easy answers.

Psalm 91:1-2 "He who dwells in the secret place of the Most High shall abide under the shadow of the Almighty."

I wasn't raised in a Christian family. I only became a Christian a year ago. How can I be a witness to my family?

The desire of God is that every person come to a place where they accept Him and His son, Jesus Christ. That is not going to happen to all humanity. Many people reject what God has done for them. I am glad you have chosen to become part of the family of God. This relationship will have benefits for you that will become a source of strength to you.

1. The most difficult people to witness to are family members, probably because they know us best and watch our lives the closest. God knows you want to see your family come to salvation, so as you seek Him, He will build into you a heart that is sensitive to each of your family members.

2. You can not make them receive what has brought joy into your life.

3. You should develop a systematic way of praying for your family members to help you remember to pray for them consistently.

4. The fruit of your life will be the greatest witness of all. Your family should be able to see how God is interacting in your life and how you are changing into a different person. Your joy should be evident and there should be a peace in your life that is obvious to anyone who knows you, especially your family.

5. You have taken on a great responsibility. The slightest discrepancy in your behavior and attitude may be all that is needed to give your family another excuse to reject Christ.

6. Be real. A genuine Christian is contagious. Loving Jesus becomes a natural part of who you are and when you are sold out for Christ, the people around you will notice the difference in your life.

7. Don't be discouraged when your family is nonresponsive. God's time table is not yours and they must respond to Him or reject Him.

II Corinthians 2:14-16 "Now thanks be to God who always leads us in triumph in Christ and through us diffuses the fragrance of His knowledge in every place. For we are to God the fragrance of Christ to those that are being saved and to those that are perishing. To one we are the aroma of death to death, to the other the aroma of life to life." 188

A NOTE FROM BECKY:

My prayer for you is that you will find this Bible study challenging yet encouraging. I hope it inspires you to grow in your personal relationship with Jesus. As you grow in Christ, I pray that you come to depend on the presence of the Holy Spirit to sustain you through all the situations which you will face during your life.

Jesus loves you and wants your life to be filled with His blessings, strength and power. He provides for you and will reveal Himself to you as you seek Him.

Sometimes the only thing that gets me through a difficult day is knowing that Jesus is present with me. Knowing that He cares and wants to bless my life brings me hope to continue on and face the new uncertainties of tomorrow.

God bless you and may His peace reign in your life.

Becky H. Drace